COASTAL
NAVIGATION

GLÉNANS
GUIDES

COASTAL
NAVIGATION

Translated by Peter Davison

David & Charles

A David & Charles Book

Translation © Peter Davison, 1995
First published in French as *La Navigation Côtière*
Copyright © Éditions du Seuil, 1992
English translation, *Coastal Navigation*

First published 1995 ISBN 0 7153 0297 3

Part of this guide first appeared in
The Glénans Manual of Sailing, David & Charles, 1993.
This book was prepared by Jean-Yves Bequignon
and Jean-Louis Goldschmid. John Jameson read and
commented on the English translation.
Cartoons: Claire Dubret.
Photographs: page 141: Antoine Sézérat; pages 10, 24, 32,
52, 63, 69, 71, 73, 145: Jean-Louis Guéry; page 126:
Furuno France; page 24: Trimble navigation France SA.
All the photographs in this book are held in the Glénans
photographic library and were taken by members of the
Glénans committee.
Maps: Service Hydrographique et Océanographique de la
Marine (SHOM).

A catalogue record of this book is available from the British Library

ISBN 0 7153 0297 3

Typeset by XL Publishing Services, Nairn
and printed in Italy by LEGO SpA
for David & Charles
Brunel House Newton Abbot Devon

CONTENTS

I am delighted to take this opportunity to add a few words to this new book on coastal navigation, because safety at sea is a joint concern of the Glénans sailing school and of my society, the French national lifeboat society.

The risk of losing human life at sea is certainly reduced by having lifeboats at regular intervals around the coast, capable of swift reaction to emergencies. But safety at sea begins with prevention, and with training. The more mission reports I read from our lifeboat crews the more I am convinced that better theoretical and practical understanding of the sea and its dangers would have avoided so many accidents.

The national lifeboat society exists to save life. Over the last thirty years there has been a major change in the type of vessel we are called on to assist. Thirty years ago, most of our distress calls came from merchant shipping. Today, 80% of the 2700 vessels to whose calls we respond are pleasure craft. Most of those sailing these boats are well trained (and the Glénans school can take pride in its contribution to this) but there are still too many who venture afloat without observing elementary precautions. The engine breaks down, navigational errors are made, the weather forecast is not taken seriously... and you have a recipe for disaster.

*T*here is no such thing as perfect safety, and not every risk can be avoided. But give yourself a good chance by studying a few pages of theory and then try putting that theory into practice. The practice will help the theory make sense. Read this excellent little book over and over again: it will help, too.

*S*ailing round our coasts is a pleasure and an art. All those who are learning or continuing to sail should master the art, because mastery gives one confidence and joy in setting out to sea.

Admiral Yves Leenhardt
President, Société Nationale
de Sauvetage en Mer
(the French equivalent of the
Royal National Lifeboat Institution)

*N*avigation, in its restricted sense, means simply the techniques used to find one's position at sea, choose a route and check that one is following the chosen route.

*T*his definition should not be taken to imply that navigation is needed only by those taking to the high seas. In reality, the moment you leave the shore then turn round to check how far you have gone, you are navigating. In a dinghy, there are only a few cases where you really need to navigate (such as deciding which side to go up a long beat). On a day cruiser or a fishing boat, you need a little more knowledge: how to spot landmarks and use them, taking account of tides and currents, how to use a compass and a chart.

*F*or the sort of coastal cruising we are talking about, this is not enough. You will need to use more complex methods and instruments to take bearings and choose a course and you will need to be able to fix your own position. This is serious navigation, basically no different from that needed by ocean-going yachts (except that offshore, one relies on radio signals and the stars to steer by). The book is written from the point of view of the coastal cruiser who is just as likely to be bay-hopping as spending a day or so out of sight of land. As our vessel, we have chosen our own training boat, the 7·60m Glénans.

We have two main aims. The first is to show the differences between theory and practice, especially when the practice is limited by a small cabin. On dry land, it is easy to be clever; but the best technique in the world cannot be said to have proved itself until it has helped you out in uncomfortable conditions. This is why we have generally opted for simple solutions, with checks built in to help avoid gross mistakes. Occasionally there is a more refined technique shown, but you will readily appreciate that most of these are designed for use in fair weather.

Our second aim is to reduce theory to a bare minimum, backing it up or even replacing it with concrete examples. Navigational technique is less a set of rules than a way of looking at the world, a logical system, a set of necessary learned responses for the world of the boat. However sophisticated and precise your new electronic gadget, you must never let it elbow aside your own critical faculties; and the information it gives you will in any case only make sense if you know the basics already. This is why, in our handbook, you will find traditional sayings, protractor-rulers and home-made logs alongside explanations of way points, Decca and Global Positioning Systems.

Satellite navigation has moved on so fast in the last few years that it really does force us to look at our techniques anew. The price of the gear is coming down all the time, and in a very few years, it will be part of the boat's standard equipment. The task we face is to recognise this progress, while not reducing the sailor to a pusher of buttons who is lost as soon as the battery goes flat. Rather than a computer-driven navigation system, we have therefore aimed for a computer-assisted navigation system (CAN for short).

*S*ome of our examples will be quite complicated. They show the requirements of the navigator's art: rigour and imagination, prudence and daring, humility and obstinacy. Some people develop a passion for this art: it becomes a sort of 'total' discipline, combining mathematics and poetry rather than setting them against each other, using them together to choose a route and to understand more fully the land and sea all around.

GLÉNANS 7·60

The Glénans 7·60 design was launched in 1991. It has taken the place of our Mousquetaires and Tonic 23s as the small cruiser in the Glénans school fleet. It is designed as a teaching yacht, but is faster and much more modern than its predecessors.

LOA: 7·60m
LWL: 6·80m · Number 2 jib: 13sq m
Beam: 2·83m · Number 3 jib: 9sq m
Draft: 1·25m · Storm jib: 3sq m
Displacement: 2000kg · Spinnaker: 35-40sq m
Build material: fibreglass · Genoa: 16sq m
Keel: 630kg · Engine: Lambardini LDW 401 M (9 PS)
Sail area: 32sq m · Bunks: 5
Mainsail: 16sq m · Designer: Yves Guignot

1

NAVIGATION EQUIPMENT

Navigation equipment includes all instruments for measuring something, and they are generally fragile and expensive. You should spend time working out where to locate them.

Instruments which are hand held need a storage place which is well shielded from knocks but at the same time handy, so you will always stow them in the correct spot after use. Fixed instruments need to be shielded from knocks and some need to be kept in a dry place.

As the chart table is invaded over time by ever more sophisticated instruments, each one a better and more powerful electronic equivalent of some traditional tool of the sailor's trade, it becomes ever more necessary to instal them properly.

There are now available integrated electronic navigation systems. The integrated electronic navigator can work out everything for you, from where you are to when you will arrive. Wonderful though this facility can be, it needs to be treated with caution and realism.

On-board electronics

You need to have the manual equivalent on board of every electronic instrument: a leadline, for instance, and not just the echo sounder.

These aids to navigation do no more than give precise measurements of their dedicated parameter: boat speed for the log, wind speed for the anemometer. The measurements cannot replace the knowledge of what these measurements mean, and you should not put your faith in them to the extent that you lose the ability to check them for yourself.

All electronic instruments use electricity, some more than others. A boat which is well equipped with electronic wizardry needs a reliable source of power. It is always possible that some accident might deprive you of all your electricity, and you must ensure that such an accident does not cripple the navigator.

The installation of electronic instruments needs to be carried out with considerable care, using plated copper wire to attach them to the power source. The instruments need to be protected from knocks and from salt water – whether the water comes from contact with wet fingers or some other source. They are best installed, therefore, at ceiling level, with their buttons and keys protected by transparent plastic sheeting.

Any wires running between the instruments themselves and their displays need to be all in one piece, with no junctions, and protected from wear. The best way of protecting them is to pass them through conduits, for instance down the inside of the mast, and to make sure they do not run through the bilges.

Compass

A compass gives direction relative to magnetic north. It is made of one or more magnets fixed on a circular plate, the compass rose, marked from 0° to 360°, pivoted at the centre and floating in a liquid in a closed bowl. Depending on the type of compass, this liquid can be oil, white spirit, glycerine or a water/alcohol mix.

The magnets follow the direction of the Earth's magnetic field (or, to be precise, they follow its horizontal component!) and the rose markings are arranged such that 0° points to magnetic north.

Steering compass
The steering compass is aligned with the axis of the boat, shown as a line (the lubber line or centreline) drawn on the compass bowl. This allows the helm to read off the boat's course directly from the alignment of this line with the rose markings. The compass is hung in gimbals so that the rose stays horizontal.

There are several types of steering compass:
The **traditional compass** is very simple and therefore cheap. One can read off one's course at any time, but one needs to keep the really rather faint degree markings in line with the lubber line, which can be inconvenient. This type of compass is really only usable if it is divided into the thirty-two points of the compass as well as having the degree markings. This way, the markings will be clearer.

The **domed compass** works on the same principles as the traditional compass but has several lubber lines marked and a domed top glass which

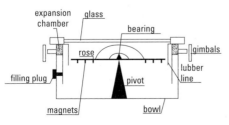

expansion chamber · glass · bearing · gimbals · rose · lubber line · filling plug · pivot · magnets · bowl

magnifies the markings for the helm who is in line with one or other of the lubber lines. This type of compass is particularly useful on large yachts, but of little interest for small-boat sailors, as it can be fragile and one does need space to move around to get the best effect from the magnification of the lubber lines.

The **vertical reading bulkhead compass** is widespread and extremely convenient. There are generally two, sited one on each side of the cockpit bulkhead. The lubber line is marked at the back of the bowl, so the helm needs to read off the markings the other way round from normal compasses.

The **fluxgate compass** is found on steel and reinforced concrete boats. The compass can be insulated from the magnetic properties of the hull by siting the instrument itself up the mast, with a display by the helm. These compasses are expensive.

The **simple compass** is one which is not mounted on gimbals and probably fairly small: it is perfectly adequate (and actually very useful) for small boats.

Installation

A compass should be installed as far away as possible from any metal on board, and in particular away from any variable magnetic fields such as those created by the radio, any loudspeakers, radio direction-finding devices, other compasses and any switch gear. It should of course be in a place where it will not be clouted regularly by winch handles, and it deserves its own cover for when it is not in use.

Unless the compass is beyond the influence of other magnetic fields, it will deviate from magnetic north. This can be compensated by a specialist who will place further magnets around the compass rose to offset the local fields. A further step, if compensation is insufficient, is known as adjusting the compass.

A domed compass must be placed so that the helm has one of the lubber lines in sight. An ordinary compass also needs to be easily in view of the helm, but its position is less critical. Any fixed compass must not be masked by the crew as they sit in the cockpit or move around the boat.

Lighting

The compass should be lit moderately: if the light is too strong it will blind the helm. It is therefore best to use a low-wattage light bulb, preferably red. Most compasses have the correct built-in lighting. We advise strongly against using a pocket torch to light the compass: the batteries will not necessarily be antimagnetic, even if they look like plastic. You will most likely have a false reading while you hold the torch close to the compass, then the compass will return to its true reading when it is back in darkness …

Maintenance

A compass does not need much maintenance, but you do need to remember to keep the gimbals lubricated. If a bubble appears in the liquid, turn the compass upside down for a moment then bring it slowly back upright. If this does not get rid of the bubble, you will need to get extra liquid added by an expert or the manufacturer (or add it yourself if you are certain what sort of liquid it is).

Hand-bearing compass

This is an ordinary compass which is held in the hand and which has a built-in prism which allows you to see the bearing displayed as you look along the lubber line. Although this is a hand-held compass, it is not designed to withstand knocks: it must be kept in a pocket or in its own compartment, not left in a corner somewhere 'temporarily' or worn around your neck like a pendant.

If the hand-bearing compass is battery-lit, make sure you use anti-magnetic batteries. Check that they are antimagnetic by running them around the edge of the compass and watching the reactions of the rose. Check each battery, as even two batteries of the same type might well have different characteristics.

Since a hand-bearing compass is mobile, it cannot be adjusted in the way that a fixed compass can be. Compensation only works for a specific, precise position. If your boat is made of steel or concrete, you will need a fixed bearing compass. The alternative is to use an azimuth bearing ring, which will not measure the bearing of the landmark, but will give you the angle between the boat's centre axis and the direction of the mark.

This hand-bearing compass is easy to use as the bearing is read off from a focal point at infinity, allowing you to focus on the mark at the same time as reading the bearing, if you keep both eyes open.

Log

The boat's speed and thus the distance covered can be measured by using an item called a log. The log is generally an electronic instrument, but it is also easy to make your own simple Dutchman's log, which works in just the same way as an old-fashioned ship's log.

Electronic logs

This is a sort of distance counter operated by a slotted rotating drum or paddle wheel underneath the hull. The turns are counted electronically and the speed and distance covered are displayed on a screen by the chart table and/or by the helm. The readings given are usually accurate to within half a knot to one knot.

The sensor needs to be situated forward of the keel, close to the centreline of the boat, with the rotor blades or paddles some 2-4cm out from the hull so that they are not affected by the boundary layer.

The blades must be retractable so that they can be cleaned of any flotsam that might upset their functioning. Keep your foot over the hole while you are cleaning them! It is crucial to get the wheel pointing in the right direction, so that the maximum speed is achieved. The log can be wired straight in to the electronic navigator, so that the navigator does not miss out on any information.

Ship's log

This is a flat piece of wood, ballasted so that it floats vertically, and attached to a line by a span. Knots are tied in the line at intervals of 7·71m/25ft 4in (ie 1/240 of a nautical mile). The log is dropped in the water and the line let out. The knots are then counted as they slip through your hands. Your speed in knots is the number of knots that go out in 15 seconds (ie 1/240 of an hour).

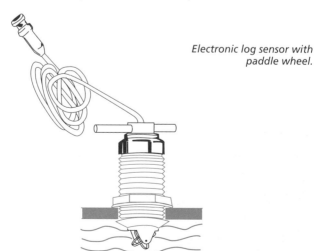

Electronic log sensor with paddle wheel.

An alternative way of measuring the speed is to measure the amount of time taken to travel a known distance. Simply make two knots in the line, say 25, 30 or 40m apart. You then measure the time taken for the second knot to slip through your hand. Since we know that 1 knot equals almost exactly 0·5m per second, the sum is simple…

■

Making a ship's log

The drogue or float. Take a piece of ply 8-10mm thick, a small wedge-shaped sliver of wood, a piece of lead sheet and join them together as in the diagram. The lead should weight the drogue so the tip sticks just out of the water with the drogue upright.

The span. Take two lengths of 3-4mm cord about 80cm long, and a clothes peg. Tie a small loop in one end of each line, put an overhand knot in the middle of the line and fix the other end through the hole in the wedge at the top corner of the drogue. The other length of line should be fed through the spring of the clothes peg and fixed there with a figure-of-eight knot either side of the spring. Both free ends should be fed through the bottom holes of the drogue and tied off.

Now feed the top line through the gap in the clothes peg so it is above the overhand stop knot. This should then give a collapsible log (useful when you want to pull it in, since a single sharp upward tug on the line will snap the line through the peg and collapse the span).

The line. Use a 2-3mm line at least 70m long (or longer if you plan on sailing that fast …). A loop on the end, big enough to fit the drogue through, will allow you to fix the line easily to the span.

The first knot in the line should be about 10m above the drogue, and subsequent knots should theoretically be 7·71m apart. In practice, 7·5m is about right, as there is always a certain amount of drag as the line is let out. If you tie a tuft of wool in each knot, with a different colour for each, you should be able to read off your speed that much more quickly. As the log is pulled back in, drop the line into a bucket fixed to the aft pulpit.

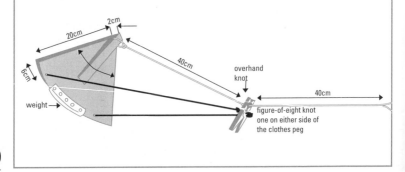

The ship's log is not only simple to make, it actually gives reliable results. Use yours to check the accuracy of your electronic log.

$$V = \frac{2d}{t}$$

V = Velocity in knots
d = distance covered in metres
t = time in seconds

Better still, and cheaper

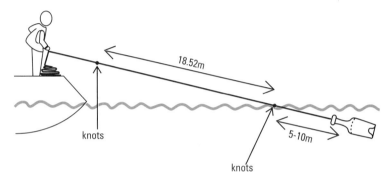

Emergency log
When in need, you can make a replacement log using the leadline and a bottle nearly full of water (so that it just about floats). Let out the first few metres of line so that it is free of any turbulence created by the boat and check the time the boat takes to cover 18·52m (1/100 of a nautical mile). The approximate speed can then be found by dividing 36 (about twice the distance) by the time taken. Thus, if you take 18 seconds, your speed is 2 knots; 9 seconds means you are travelling at 4 knots; 4 seconds means 9 knots. This method is not very precise, but it's quick, simple and cheap. If you have no bottle to hand, then you really are in desperate straits, and worrying about your boat speed probably is not your prime concern!

Echo sounder

This is an electronic device which continually indicates the depth of the water, up to quite considerable values. It is particularly useful if you need to follow an underwater contour.

The echo sounder consists of an ultrasound transceiver and an antenna situated under the hull. It emits a cone of waves about 20° to 50° wide, and will generally receive echoes from the floor as much as 100m down. The minimum required for sailing around Western European coasts is 100m.

The depth is read out on a screen next to the chart table with maybe an extra display in the cockpit for those rich enough. The transceiver head needs to be placed forward of the keel so as not to pick up false echoes. The angle of heel of the boat must be less than the angle of transmission of the sounder. Otherwise, you need two transceivers, one either side of the centreline, and a mercury switch which activates the one lower down. The head needs to be kept free of weed and paint.

The echo sounder should tell you the distance between the seabed and the sounder head, but this point is worth checking.

The echo sounder
The sounder head must be:
■ *always submerged;*
■ *some way from the keel;*
■ *and its cone should be kept as close to the vertical as possible.*
The picture shows a number of errors!

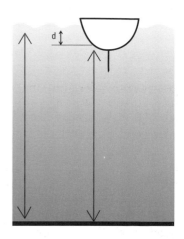

In theory, to work out the depth of water, one needs to take into account the distance d between the sounder and the waterline. In practice, it is better to add the total draught of the boat to the sounder readout: this gives you a certain margin of error.

The leadline

Manual sounding is carried out with a lead weight of 0·5 to 1kg and a line about 50m long, with depth markings. Ideally the weight should have a slightly concave bottom; you can then put some grease in it and take a sample from the bottom, or at least check that it did reach bottom.

Mark the line with indelible marker ink, with one colour for every 10m (one stroke for 10m, 2 for 20, etc.) and another for the 5m intervals (one at 15m, 2 at 25, etc.). Only the first 10m need to be marked with individual metres. Do not forget that the line will stretch as you are heaving the lead, so be sure to do your marking with the line taut.

The leadline (or plumbline) can be kept in a bucket, a bag or a basket. It must be tied to the bottom of its container and flaked carefully. If you throw it in a heap or try to coil it, it is bound to tie itself in knots. Most boats need only a leadline. All boats should have one, since the electronic echo sounder (a) can break down, and (b) cannot tell you about the nature of the sea bed.

Barometer

'Stop tapping my face, I'm doing my best. And please don't attach me to the cockpit bulkhead or I'll get shaken to bits!'

It is highly desirable for the barometer to show the correct pressure, so you can compare your local conditions with the larger picture given on the radio. To calibrate the barometer, jot down its reading at six o'clock in the morning or evening, then compare this with the reading given the next day in the newspaper for the same time. Move the barometer needle by the amount of the difference, using the little screw on the back. Check it again the next day.

Radio receivers

Boats which will not venture more than sixty miles from land need only a simple transistor radio to listen to long- and short-wave transmissions. This will give you the broadcasts of the BBC and France Inter, as well as regional weather bulletins.

Anyone who will be sailing further out to sea needs to be able to listen in by VHF radio to the specialist maritime stations which transmit on the Single Side Band between 1·6 and 4MHz. Any receiver which bears the letters A3J or J3E can pick out these stations.

Your radio reception will be much improved by the addition of a good aerial. This will stop you needing to turn the transistor round for long wave stations, and will drastically improve your SSB reception. A backstay (suitably insulated top and bottom) makes an excellent aerial. On metal boats, you will need an earth.

For radio direction finding, you need to be able to receive radio beacons which transmit on around 300KHz, and you need a mobile aerial which has a compass attached so that you can take a bearing on the transmitter. The aerial can be linked into your main radio system, or into its own dedicated receiver which is much simpler.

Any radio equipment needs its own stowage, preferably out of the way of water and knocks. The radio should be some distance from the compass, because the loudspeakers have a large magnet inside them. The radio direction finder needs to be stored somewhere safe but quickly accessible: it is even more fragile than your hand bearing compass and should be stowed the moment it is no longer in use.

Radio transmitters

Many pleasure boat sailors have a transmitter on board so that they can make contact with the land and with other boats. Short distance

VHF communication systems are improving as their price is coming down. A portable system may be had for less than £400, and will allow you to transmit over a radius of several miles or several tens of miles depending on the height of your aerial.

Theoretically, two portable sets 2m above sea level can communicate over a distance of 6·5 miles; or each can communicate with a coastal station 100m above sea level from 25 miles away. With a powerful transmitter, a fixed masthead aerial and an appropriate budget, you can use the system as you would your own phone.

VHF radio is not exactly a safety device, but it can fulfil some safety-related functions which contribute considerably to your comfort:

■ distress signals can be sent out on channel 16;

■ other boats can be asked for assistance;

■ medical advice, weather forecasts and port information may be obtained;

■ radio telephone contact can be maintained with home base;

■ in certain cases, one can obtain information on one's own position.

A simple 4- or 5-channel handset, protected by a watertight pouch, is adequate for asking passers-by for a tow, drawing attention to oneself and communicating with other boats in your flotilla. The handset can also be taken with you in the dinghy should you need to abandon the boat. You should have a rechargeable battery and charger, but you need a couple of spare batteries as well. You need a battery charge indicator to tell whether your set is capable of transmitting or not. If you are going a long way and you absolutely must stay in touch with land, you need an SSB transceiver. This sort of equipment is expensive and quite demanding to operate, and lies outside the scope of this book.

Important: Make sure you have an adequate source of electricity for all the electronic items you plan to run on board. They are quite draining on a battery, and you should ensure that they are not used excessively, both for your own good and for the good of others who need to use the same frequency.

Wind direction and speed instruments

These two pieces of equipment are generally combined in one assembly at the masthead. They are expensive, and usually found only on the best-equipped boats. Buying them is really only justified if you plan to race a lot.

They give an exact reading, undisturbed by the effect of the rig, so long as the sea is relatively calm and the wind relatively constant. When the boat is rolling in a heavy sea with light winds, there are too many variables for the equipment to give a reliable reading.

An alternative, yet effective windsock can be constructed out of 1·5m of steel wire and a length of spinnaker cloth!

Sextant

The sextant is an optical instrument for measuring angles very precisely. It is used for measuring the angle between any two points, which in coastal navigation means the angle between two landmarks. Hence its appearance in this chapter.

Micrometer sextant.

Theory

A lens and a small mirror are fixed on a frame which is shaped like an arc of a circle. The arc is marked from 0° to 120° and toothed. A large movable mirror, the index mirror, travels along the arc. The index mirror is moved by a lever called the index and adjusted by a micrometer screw which is marked in minutes and tenths of minutes. The smaller mirror is most often a piece of highly reflective transparent glass.

Maintenance

Sextants are fragile and must not be given even the slightest knock. The sextant should be regularly lubricated by wiping it with cotton wool with a small amount of Vaseline. It must be kept in its box, away from water. Older models of sextant have such fine graduations on the arc that it is best not to touch the arc at all.

Plastic sextants

Plastic sextants have been on the market for a number of years. They are nowhere near so precise as metal sextants, as they bend a little, but nor are they so expensive. If you take a few precautions in use, they can manage good measurements which are correct to within a few minutes. This is generally as accurate as one needs.

The precautions which should be borne in mind are:

■ to take the sextant out of the cabin at least ten minutes before you plan to use it, and hold it by its handle throughout. This will ensure that all parts of the sextant are at the same temperature by the time it is used;

■ to hold the handle as lightly and with as constant pressure as possible, so as to minimise any distortion;

■ to check the index error before every observation;
■ to use it just as you would a metal sextant;
■ to check the index error again after the observation, if desired.

If the error found is approximately the same as that found earlier, use the average of the two values as the correction factor in your calculation. If it is a long way from the previous reading, start the whole procedure again.

Electronic navigation

Satellite navigation

The receiver picks up information from the satellites of the TRANSIT or GPS systems which are in orbit round the earth. The electronic navigator uses one or more sightings to plot your longitude and latitude. If you then feed in your speed and heading, either by hand or

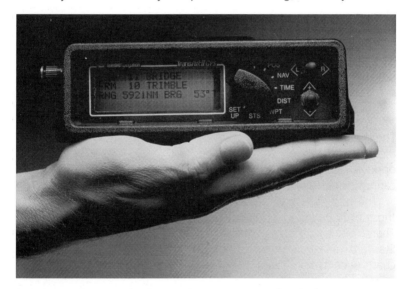

by plugging it into the log and compass, it will calculate your position constantly. It can also calculate the course required to a given way point, estimate the time required to get there, and perform many other useful functions.

Hyperbolic navigation systems

These systems cover a given limited area of sea, outside which your machine cannot be used. They pick up a signal every 10-30 seconds and constantly update your position; they then use the stored information to calculate your average heading and course made good over a given period: three, five or ten minutes depending on what you need. A hyperbolic navigation system can also estimate an arrival time, calculate the best moment to tack, etc., so long as the operator spends a little time exploring all its facilities. Incidentally, seasickness is the source of most navigation mistakes …

All this wizardry is wonderful, but one must also know how to navigate manually.

Navigation by computer

A computer on board is like an extra crew member permanently dedicated to letting you know where the boat is, where it should be heading, when it is best to tack, how far off the direct course you are, how fast you are sailing, how deep the water is, what time lunch will be ready…

Staggering, really.

A sufficiently powerful computer adequately programmed can perform all these functions if it is hooked up to the necessary sensors: log, wind indicators, navigator, electric compass, radar – if you have one – and electronic weather map decoder. This can save the skipper an awful lot of headaches. There are specialised programmes (such as Mac Sea on the Apple Macintosh) to do all this. One can even feed in electronic charts of the sea area you are covering and the computer then takes on the job of pilot as well!

Charts and documents

The member of your crew who is responsible for navigation will be recording all the information gathered on a nautical chart (as opposed to a land map, which some people use but which really cannot be recommended).

The best charts are Admiralty charts or their French equivalent, those of SHOM (Service Hydrographique et Océanique de la Marine). There are commercially published alternatives such as those of Stanford or Imray, which have different graphical symbols. Paper charts such as these are vulnerable to water. The charts of the areas most widely used by pleasure boat sailors are published on plastic, which is greatly preferable to paper if it can be found for the area you are interested in. To draw on plastic-covered charts you need a soft pencil, 2B or 3B, or a dry laboratory pencil, such as All Stabilo 8008.

Caring for your charts

Charts are fragile and expensive. They need to be looked after if they are to remain legible. If you do not have space to store the charts flat, they are best rolled. Unrolling them can involve some acrobatics, but it is better than folding, as they quickly become illegible and tear at the folds. If you must fold a chart, choose where to fold it, where the folds will matter less. Do not just fold it down the middle.

Tears in charts can be repaired by gluing a sheet of old chart paper onto the back, using ordinary office glue. Sticky tape is not recommended, as it tends to shrink slightly after it has been stretched onto the paper, and makes the chart wrinkle.

Storing paper charts

On a long cruise, it is worth storing several charts together by area, so that you group them eg as 'western Channel, west of Cherbourg', or 'northern Spain, St.-Jean-de-Luz to La Coruña'. All you actually keep on the table is a list of which charts you have in store; or better still, the general map of the region divided up and numbered into the individual charts and the areas they cover.

■

Admiralty chart formats

Chart format	paper size
Half DE (unfolded chart)	*711 × 521mm*
DE (single-folded chart)	*1041 × 711mm*
Long DE (double-folded chart)	*1270 × 711mm*
A0	*1189 × 841mm*

2

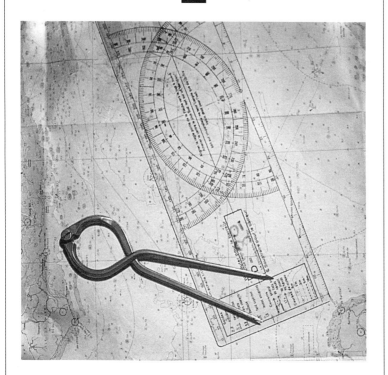

SEAMARKS
AND
PUBLICATIONS

Nobody is going to embark on a voyage around the world with nothing but a pipe and a penknife for luggage: naturally enough, a certain amount of knowledge is necessary. First of all, one must be able to use and recognise the various sorts of reference points available: buoys and beacons, lights, sound signals, radio signals and the stars. Thanks to them, it is quite simple to measure and maintain one's current distance from land. Another distance must also be known: that of the keel from the seabed. To do this, it is necessary to be able to calculate the tides in order to be able to say how deep the water will be in a given place and at a given time; one should also know about the tidal streams that are associated with the ebb and flow of the sea.

Apart from the buoyage systems, whose rules can be learned by heart with little difficulty, none of the different reference points can be used without the various documents which describe both them and their position. The most important references are the *Macmillan and Silk Cut Nautical Almanac*, the *Macmillan and Silk Cut Yachtsman's Handbook*, *Reed's Nautical Almanac*, the *Cruising Association Handbook*, Admiralty Pilots, and the Admiralty *List of Lights and Fog Signals*, and *List of Radio Signals*.

In this chapter we will go through the different land and sea marks, as well as the various reference works, along with the documents and charts that should be used in conjunction with them. This will give an overview of an otherwise rather difficult subject, and will give the reader a starting point. If a more complete guide is required, then the reader is directed to *Reed's* or *Macmillan's* almanacs (the French equivalent is the SHOM's *Guide du Navigateur*) which contain all the information that one could wish to have at one's disposal, and much more that one would never need or, indeed, know what to do with.

The first, and one of the most important things to bear in mind is the fact that the world described by these documents changes from day to day. Even the most official documents are unusable, and should therefore not be used under any circumstances, unless they have been rigorously kept up to date. We shall therefore describe how this is to be done for each of the works the navigator will be required to use. In the first place, it would, however, perhaps be of some use to give the reader an idea of the organisation set up to provide all this information.

■

How to get up to date at the start of the season

It is rare for anyone to keep meticulously up to date with the various changes and notices pertaining to navigation that are published over the winter. However, it is perfectly possible to find out everything that one needs to know without too much difficulty if one takes the following steps:

■ Most publishers of reference works produce regular supplements to update their information. The major almanacs are in any case annual.

■ The Admiralty *Notices to Mariners* are published weekly and give essential updates to Admiralty charts. They are available from Admiralty Chart Agents or can be consulted at harbourmasters' offices. There is a special *Small Craft Edition* of *Notices to Mariners* published periodically, which summarises the most relevant information for pleasure sailors.

Maritime information

According to the *Guide du Navigateur* (the French equivalent of the Admiralty Pilots, or *Reed's*), navigational information can take four forms depending on the degree of urgency involved:

■ Basic information is to be found in the relevant publications and the corrections to these supplied by the publisher.

■ 'Normal' information is classed as useful but non-urgent, and not pertaining to matters that would place the safety of the crew in question. It is published every week in small pamphlets entitled *Notices to Mariners*, or, for cruising in France, *Groupes hebdo-madaires d'avis aux navigateurs* (Weekly update for navigators). These pamphlets contain, along with a variety of other information, the latest changes and corrections made to the basic documents, and summary tables of corrections and notices.

■ Immediate information includes things which could affect the safety of the navigator in the short or medium term. In France bulletins known by the acronym DIFRAP can be consulted in any harbourmaster's office, as well as in the local press.

■ Urgent information covers events that have just occurred and which could put the navigator at considerable and immediate risk: light gone out, buoy disappeared, drifting wreck etc. This is broadcast by radio in the form of urgent information for navigators at fixed times by the coastal stations. Details of the bulletins are also posted in all harbourmasters' offices, sometimes in the yacht club and generally in the local newspapers and guides.

This system should, in principle, save the navigator from any nasty surprises. However, despite the remarkable work that they do (and with very limited resources, it has to be said), those who produce published information defer to the knowledge and experience of every navigator in deciding how much confidence to place in a given piece of information. Any publisher will be pleased to receive feedback on the accuracy of their reference material (indeed they specifically request it, ensuring that their address is prominently printed, for this purpose) and if you ever find errors or omissions in pilots or almanacs, you must consider it your duty to other yachts to report these errors.

The buoyage system

Our ancestors were blessed with both good eyes and keen noses. The only reference points available to them were those that lay along the coast itself. It may well have been that the sighting of a particular monument, such as a tumulus, a menhir, an ancient temple, a watchtower, or even a particular rock or clump of trees might have been all they needed to guide them safely home to their village.

Nowadays, landmarks, that is to say fixed visible points along the coast, are equally precious to us. Simply take into account the fact that the landscape is changing a little faster than before. Steeples, water towers or factory chimneys, which once were useful guides to navigation, can be hidden from view by trees or, more frequently, the apparently unstoppable progress of civilisation.

Now, only official landmarks provide a reliable guide: white-washed rocks, lighthouses, etc, all noted in the relevant publications. These are very carefully maintained and kept safe from the unwelcome attention of developers.

Landmarks are not part of the system of beacons per se. Instead, the term buoyage is a blanket term covering all the markers put in place by Trinity House (in France, the Service des Phares et Balises) for the use of navigators. Those items that come under the general

33

heading of buoyage are the buoys, stone towers and beacons properly so called, which are perches set into the rock, or fixed to the sea bed.

How to recognise a mark

Every buoy and mark has a precise purpose, indicated by their shape, colour and topmark, and often by a light on top.

The shape (cone, cylinder, sphere, spar or pillar) is not sufficient on its own to identify the mark. There is no strict code, and a good number of the small beacons predate such rules as exist.

The colour (red, green, black, yellow) is much more important. A rust-red colour simply means that the mark is badly maintained, but this is rare in Europe.

The topmark (cone, cylinder, sphere or cross), should settle any doubts that still remain after one has made a note of the colour of the buoy, because it gives precise indications which complement those given by the colour.

In 1976, there were about thirty beacon systems in operation throughout the world, but since 1982 a single system has been established as standard. In this, there are two main types of marks: lateral and cardinal, and also three other types. See the flap inside the back cover for a summary.

Lateral marks

Lateral marks are to be found in channels and at the entry to ports. They are laid out so as to help a navigator entering harbour. When leaving harbour, their meaning is reversed. The principle is as follows:

34

■ any green marker, topped with a conical topmark point upwards and a green light, must be left to starboard;

■ any red marker with a cylindrical or can-shaped topmark and a red light must be left to port.

These markers are usually numbered. The numbering starts out to sea. The red markers have even numbers, and the green markers, odd numbers.

All of this is fairly easy to remember. However, if your memory is a bit shaky, the following mnemonic may help:

PORT is a RED drink, and should be LEFT. It is also helpful to bear in mind that the colour of the lights corresponds to the lights on the boat: red to port, green to starboard.

In certain coastal rivers, the markers are covered in a reflective paint, which shows up nicely when hit by a searchlight. Many buoys and towers are also equipped with a radar reflector.

When entering harbour, a yacht should leave to starboard any green mark with a conical topmark, and to port any red mark with a cylindrical topmark.

Cardinal Marks

Cardinal marks – so named because they refer to the cardinal points – are used to mark dangerous spots along the coast, as well as some dangerous areas at sea. The principle is as follows: a cardinal mark defines its own position in relation to the blackspot, and therefore indicates where it is safe to navigate. A southern cardinal mark is positioned to the south of the danger area, and you must therefore keep to the south of it.

35

All these marks are painted yellow and black, topped by a top-mark consisting of two black cones, one on top of the other, along with a white light. The different marks are distinguished by the distribution of colours and topmarks.

The arrangement of the north and south marks appears logical, while west and east markers are shaped so that a W or an E can be made out of their left hand side. It is easy to understand the layout of the colours on the different marks if you remember that black corresponds to the point and yellow to the base of the cones. It should further be noted that a cardinal mark covers a very specific area. The presence of a west mark, for example, means that the route is clear in the sector NW-SW, but not all the way round between north and south. Furthermore, just because you have identified a cardinal mark correctly does not mean that you can get away without looking at the map.

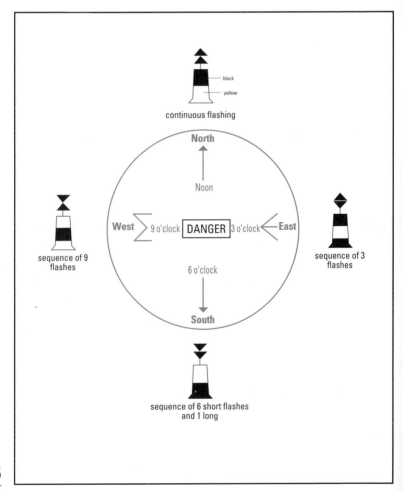

Other marks

Safe water marks

These marks indicate not the quality of the water, but whether there is any danger in the immediate vicinity. They are generally to be found at the entry to channels (for example, the buoy SN 1, which is the first marker for the channel leading into the port of Saint-Nazaire).

The markers are painted in vertical red and white stripes, sometimes topped with a red sphere (the sphere always indicates that the buoy can be passed on either side). If the buoys are marked with a light, then this is white and isophase or occulting.

Isolated danger marks

These markers indicate danger in a limited area (they are positioned directly above it). They are painted black with large red horizontal bands, carrying a characteristic topmark: two black spheres one on top of the other. If they have a light, then it is white and gives groups of two flashes.

Special marks

These mark areas set aside for particular purposes: exercises, cables etc. They are yellow, with a yellow, x-shaped topmark, and sometimes a yellow light.

See the inside back flap for illustrations of all these marks.

Lights and signals

Under the heading of lights come lighthouses, light-vessels, beacons and buoys. At night, these lights provide a very simple and clear indication of the coastline, the position of channels and so on. In fact, it is often easier to make a landfall by night than by day. The positions and characteristics of the various lights are defined in the *List of Lights*. On charts, they are shown as magenta-coloured teardrop marks, and are given a brief description. Lights are distinguished by their colour and type, the rhythm of their flashes and the time between them.

Colour
Green, red or white for ordinary buoyage. Yellow for special markers, or even bluey-white or violet in some cases.

Type
The principal sorts are: fixed lights, flashing lights, occulting lights, isophase lights and quick flashing lights.

Lens for a group flashing two flashes.

■ Fixed lights: continuous light of constant intensity

■ Flashing lights: the flashes are much briefer than the intervals in between

■ Occulting lights: periods of darkness (occultations) are much shorter than the periods of light

■ Isophase lights: the periods of darkness and lights are of equal length

■ Quick flashing lights: isophase lights with a very rapid rhythm (more than forty flashes a minute). Quick flashing lights can be either interrupted or continuous.

Rhythm

The division between periods of darkness and periods of light gives the rhythm of the light. In the case of occulting lights, there are three sorts of rhythm:

■ The periods of brightness between each occultation are always of the same duration. The light is then said to be regular, with 1 occultation: an example is the light on the green tower at Port-Louis (green light, 1 occultation, 4 seconds).

■ The occultations are separated by briefer flashes of light and grouped in twos, threes or fours, with a longer period of light separating each group. The light at Les Moutons, for example has 2 occultations.

■ The occultations are grouped irregularly, an example being Trévignon (3+1 occultations). The grouped occultations are separated from one another by shorter flashes of light, and these groups are then

Lens for light visible through 360°. Unlike the light shown above, this lens does not rotate: the rhythm is created by switching the bulb on and off. It can therefore function as an occulting, a flashing, quick-flashing or isophase light.

38

separated from the single occultation by a longer flash. The principle is the same for flashing lights.

Period
The period is the time taken for the light to go through one complete sequence of flashes, for example the Trévignon light has a period of twelve seconds from the first occultation of the group of three to the first occultation of the next group of three, or from the first isolated occultation to the next one, and so on.

Special lights
There are a certain number of lights with special characteristics:

■ Lights with sectors do not show the same colour in all directions. Each colour covers a particular area. Often, white indicates the clear area (a channel leading into a port, for example), while red and green sector lights indicate danger. But this is not always the case, and you should check the relevant charts in each case.

■ Directional lights are generally placed along the line of a channel (as with the Beuzec lights at the entry to Concarneau). These lights have a highly focused beam and are much less bright to the sides than along the line they mark.

■ Leading lights are laid out to lead the navigator along a line, as their name implies (take, for example, the lights at la Croix, or the Beuzec lights at Concarneau). The light nearer the navigator is the lower light, the light further away is the upper light .

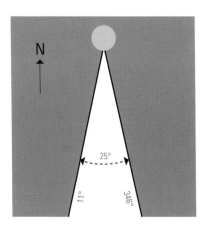

The bearings of light sectors are given from seawards. The sector shown (346° to 11°) sweeps an area to the south of the light.

■ Exit and entry lights are to be found outside ports to which there is no permanent access (because of locks, large cargo ships, or closure on certain days). These lights are always made up of a combination of red and green lights (flags during daytime). Consult the Pilot Book.

■ Auxiliary lights are based on the same structure as the main light (as at Penfret) and cover an isolated danger or indicate a passageway. These lights are not very powerful, and can only be seen from a short distance away.

Another kind of light that deserves a mention is the alternating light, which shows colour changes along the same bearing, an example being the Guernsey breakwater. There are also Air Obstruction lights which are switched on as needed and which give out a letter of the Morse code (Portsmouth, Cherbourg, Biarritz). Last but not least, there are certain lights with sectors that do not change colour, but rhythm instead. One of the more notable is the light on the Cape of Corrubedo, not too far from Cape Finisterre; this light shows 3 red flashes in one sector, and 3+2 red flashes in the next. It requires a good deal of attention to see which sector you are in.

How to recognise a light

In conditions of good visibility, lights give precise information. However, experience has shown that novices can nonetheless get a bit confused when dealing with them, particularly since they have the unfortunate tendency to take the first light they see for the one they want to see.

To identify a light, do not start out by assuming that it is the one you are looking for, and then fit the facts to suit. Instead, calmly check the characteristics first, and then identify it.

The colour ought to be obvious. However, in foggy weather, white lights can appear reddish. It is easy to identify a light's type when dealing with flashing and quick flashing lights. However, some fixed lights can be drowned out by the lights from a town. Some occulting lights can look as if they are isophase, and vice-versa. In order to work out the duration of the periods of light and dark, the best way is to count in your head (any speed will do, but counting quickly usually gives a more regular and accurate estimate).

The rhythm of a light can be calculated in the same way, either during periods of darkness for a flashing light, or during periods of light for an occulting one. It is rare that anyone should need to know the period of a light (in the waters around France, in a particular area, no two lights are distinguished by the period alone). If there is still cause for doubt, then the period can be measured by counting in seconds (counting A1, A2, A3 etc. will give a fairly accurate indication), or by using a timer.

FRANCE — DE LA POINTE DE PENMARCH A LORIENT 115

NUMÉROS	NOM DESCRIPTION — POSITION APPROCHÉE Lat N Long. W	ÉLÉVATION DU FOYER	PORTÉE (milles)	CARACTÈRE — PÉRIODE PHASES — SECTEURS D'ÉCLAIRAGE SIGNAUX DE BRUME — INTENSITÉ LUMINEUSE
40374 D.0944	Trévignon Tourelle carrée verte et blanche 7 m 47.47,6 3.51,3	11	B. 10 R. 7 V. 6	B. R. V. (3 + 1) Occ. 12 s ((1 ; 1) 2 fois ; (1 ; 3) 2 fois) 322 - R. - 351 - Obs. - 004 - B. - 051 - V. - 085 - B. - 092 - R. - 127
40378 D.0945	— Môle abri - Musoir Colonne blanche sommet vert 3 m 47.47,7 3.51,3	5	5	F. V. 4 s (1)
	ILE DE GROIX			
40952 D.0962	PEN-MEN - Au NW de l'île Tour carrée blanche, sommet noir 24 m 47.38,9 3.30,5	60	30 20	4 É. B. 25 s ((0,2 ; 2,8) 3 fois ; 0,2 ; 15,8) Vis. 309 - 275 (34) SIRÈNE 4 sons 60 s ((2 ; 3) 3 fois ; 2 ; 43) 0,2 M Ouest RADIOPHARE
40963	Bouée « Les Chats » Card. Sud 47.35,7 3.23,6	4	5	4 É. R. 12 s ((1 ; 1) 3 fois ; 1 ; 5) ⌐ SIFFLET

Reproduction of a page from the List of Lights (Livre des Feux).

When the characteristics of the light have been determined, then an attempt can be made to find out its name. In addition, it is a good idea to make other checks (position relative to other lights, bearings) in order to be certain. All this requires a certain amount of practice, and it is important not to miss any opportunity to gain experience in this vital skill.

The List of Lights

We are sailing in the vicinity of Concarneau and we see a green light, occultations in groups of 1 and 3, with a period of 12 seconds. We open the *List of Lights*. No possible alternative: it must be the Trévignon light. We also gain a good deal of additional information:

■ we can see a green light, but the Trévignon light presents other colours in other directions (white and red): it is a sector light.

■ the light is 11m above MHWS.

■ Its range of visibility varies according to colour and sector: white is the most brilliant, and is visible from the greatest distance, then next red and finally green. This is a nominal range, set out by the International Association of Lighthouse Authorities and is given for weather conditions allowing a visibility of 10 miles. Some other countries have different definitions. The *List of Lights* reproduces without any change figures given in foreign publications.

■ Next, there is the description of the different sectors and their limits. We read that the Trévignon light has six sectors: two red, one obscured, two white, one green. The green sector covers 34°, from 051° to 085°. Be warned: the sector bearings are given from sea-

41

wards; that is, they are the bearings a navigator would take. The green sector of Trévignon therefore covers an area to the WSW of the lighthouse (and not to the ENE, where there are lots of cute herds of cows, and the picturesque chapel of St Philibert, a gem of sixteenth-century architecture).

■ The list also gives a description of the structure carrying the light, and its height above ground level. This is very useful, because lighthouses are good landmarks by day, and it also saves having to look frantically for a tower when the light is tucked away in a house on a hill.

■ A detailed description of the phases of the light is also given. It is often very complicated and will probably confuse you more than it helps you – all in all, it's best not to read it.

■ For other lights, such as the one at Pen-a-Men, information is also given about fog signals, radio beacons and so on.

■ For the bigger lights, where the range of visibility is considerably extended, the geographical range of the light is given in italics. This gives the maximum distance at which the light can be seen beyond the visible horizon.

The geographical range depends on the height of the tide and the height of the eye of the observer (which in turn depends on the height of the person in question and the size of the boat). The geographical range marked in the book is calculated for an observer who is 4·5m above the surface of the sea at MHWS. It is rare that anyone on a yacht is so high up, but a table at the front of the book gives the relevant compensations.

Most lights are not manned, and in event of failure can therefore be out for several hours at a time. Buoys are not manned either (and the cormorants that generally live on them are not very good at maintenance). Do not therefore forget that the light on a buoy can malfunction, and that some time may pass before it is repaired, especially in bad weather.

Keeping the List of Lights up to date

The List of Lights always comes with either a booklet of corrections or replacement pages if it is being sold as a folder with removable pages. In the first instance, cut out the corrections and stick them in place on the page (remember to cross out the old directions and instructions, just in case the glue isn't up to it). If you have bought it in folder format, then simply replace the outdated pages.

In order to keep the work up to date thereafter, you must buy either the replacement pages that are put out every six months, or the pamphlet of corrections that appears every year. To keep up to date on a day to day basis, listen to the corrections given as part of the 'Urgent notices to mariners' at the end of weather forecasts from coastal stations, or consult the Notices to Mariners.

Fog signals

When buoys and lights disappear in the fog, sound signals take over. Old hands still remember the gunshots that used to be heard around the Stiff on the NW corner of France on these occasions. Guns are seldom, if ever, used any more, and the signals are today, in decreasing order of power:

■ diaphones, with a very deep note (le Creac'h at Ushant, le Guéveur on the island of Sein);
■ sirens, usually on lighthouses;
■ fog horns, at the end of harbour jetties;
■ bells and whistles on buoys.

Lighthouse sirens usually have the same pattern as the light, with a longer period (if it has three flashes every 20 seconds, the siren gives three blasts every minute). Since the bells and whistles on buoys are powered by the sea, they follow its rhythm. The characteristics of fog signals are given in the *List of Lights*.

All these signals do what they can, but in many cases you cannot expect precise information from them, especially concerning their exact position. Fog distorts sounds to the extent that a signal that is quite close can seem a long way off, and a signal that is on the right can appear to be on the left.

Having said that, sound signals can be quite useful, as a group of Mousquetaire yachts from the Glénans centre at Baltimore in Ireland discovered: they were able to go round the Fastnet rock at night in a real peasouper of a fog, without seeing the light once. The important thing in cases like this, is to check the information from the signals against frequent soundings, either by lead or echo sounder. Radio bearings are also of help.

Radio signals

There are various systems of radiosignals, and different ways of receiving them. The most common technique used by amateur sailors is DF wireless navigation which we will discuss in greater detail in the chapter on navigation offshore. Radiosignals are exactly like light signals in the way that they are used for navigation: in both cases, one must establish one's position in relation to the 'active beacons' whose characteristics are already known. Only the methods differ slightly: instead of using light as a signal and the eye to detect it, we use radiowaves, put out by radio beacons, and a radio receiver to transform the signals into sound.

Radio beacons are mentioned in the *List of Lights* when they are found in a lighthouse (which is often the case), but their characteristics are not given there. These are to be found in the Admiralty *List of Radiosignals* (in France, vol 91 of the publications of the SHOM,

43

Radiosignaux à l'usage des navigateurs). They are also to be found in various unofficial publications which we will discuss in due course.

Information on hyperbolic or satellite navigation is now practically unnecessary, since these now give points directly in terms of geographical co-ordinates, along with the times these satellites will be passing overhead for the next 24 hours. The main reference work for these therefore remains the manufacturer's instructions.

The stars

Are the stars lights or signals? This is largely down to one's own personal convictions. They are nonetheless useful points of reference, and allow for very precise navigation. *Reed's Nautical Almanac* publishes star charts for navigational purposes, and these are updated annually. In France, one can also consult the *Ephémérides Nautiques*, a large, expensive volume published every year by the Bureau des Longitudes. This work contains tables giving the position of the sun, the moon, four planets and 81 stars throughout the year, along with a variety of tables of corrections.

For navigation by the stars, we will discuss other tables which are essential for the various calculations that can be made from the data given either by *Reed's* or the *Ephémérides*. However, it should be noted that there are now calculators available which not only make the work easier, but which also replace certain parts of the *Ephémérides*.

The chart

The marine chart is the most basic of documents for the sailor. It gives a very precise graphic representation of the sea and the coasts, and also contains a great deal of information pertaining to markers, buoys, lights, tidal streams and many other things.

The basic principles of chart-reading are well known to anyone who paid any attention at all in school. Just in case you didn't, however, we'll go over the basics again.

Basic principles

Seeing that the world was really rather large, and realising that it would be a good idea to know where one was, human beings have invented a simple system of reference points, based on a sort of lattice of lines covering the globe. Some of the lines run parallel to the equator: these are called parallels or lines of latitude. In addition, there are the lines running perpendicular to the equator, and which meet at the poles: these are called meridians or lines of longitude. All one needs to do then is to choose a parallel and a meridian: any point on the globe can be found by reference to this system of co-ordinates. Its position with respect to the reference meridian defines its longitude. Latitude and longitude are measured in degrees and minutes. A degree is divided into sixty minutes, a minute into sixty seconds. However, nowadays we generally use degrees, minutes and tenths of a minute.

Latitude

The polar axis forms an angle of 90° with the plane of the equator. The equator has a latitude of 0°, and the poles have a latitude of 90° (north or south). All latitudes therefore fall between 0° and 90° north and south, and are measured by reference to the equator. Thus the latitude of Penfret Island (47° 43'N) corresponds to the angle that an imaginary straight line linking Penfret to the centre of the Earth makes with the plane of the equator.

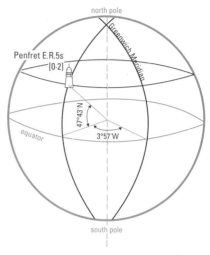

The Penfret Lighthouse is at 47° 43'N and 3° 57'W

This angle corresponds to a distance on the Earth's surface. A minute of latitude equals 1,852m. This distance is a unit of measurement known as the nautical mile. Since the Earth is not totally spherical, a minute of latitude can actually vary in length: 1,842.78m at the equator and 1,861.55m at a latitude of 85°. However, in temperate latitudes we can say:

1 minute of latitude = 1 sea mile = 1,852m.
The island of Penfret is 2,863 sea miles from the equator.

Longitude

Since there is no meridian that naturally imposes itself as a reference point, the one that passes through Greenwich has been chosen. Since the globe is divided up into 360°, longitude is counted from Greenwich (180° East, 180° West). In measures of latitude and longitude, the cardinal points are always referred to as N, S, W, and E by international convention.

The longitude of Penfret is 3° 57'W.

Distance cannot be calculated on the basis of longitude since the meridians do not run parallel to one another.

The principle of Mercator's projection is that an angle on the globe must be represented by the same angle on a chart. As a consequence, around any point, the distances on the globe and the distances on the chart are reproduced according to the same scale in all directions. There is thus no distortion when dealing with small areas. The constant distance in millimetres between any two given meridians on the chart represents a changing distance in nautical miles between the same meridians on the globe. This distance diminishes as one moves away from the Equator. As a result, the actual scale of the map increases with latitude. Large areas, such as oceans, are therefore distorted. To be more exact, the scale of Mercator's projection alters in inverse proportion to the cosine of the latitude.

Mercator's projection
The areas marked A, B, C and D all measure 15° latitude by 10° longitude. Their surface area actually diminishes as latitude increases, despite appearing to grow on the chart.

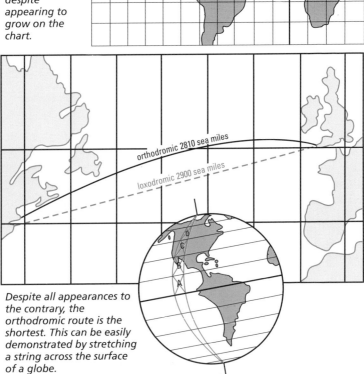

orthodromic 2810 sea miles

loxodromic 2900 sea miles

Despite all appearances to the contrary, the orthodromic route is the shortest. This can be easily demonstrated by stretching a string across the surface of a globe.

Mercator's projection

On a chart, however, the meridians are well and truly parallel to each other. The reason is that a convex surface cannot be reproduced in a plane without some distortion. Either the precise representation of angles, or an exact representation of distance must be sacrificed. As the measurement of angles is indispensable in navigation, charts are normally drawn on Mercator's projection.

On the chart, the angles are correct, but the distances are only exact at the Equator; the further one moves away from the Equator, the more exaggerated the representation is. Around the poles, the distortion is considerable: Greenland, on projections like Mercator's, seems as big as Africa, whereas it is in fact fourteen times smaller.

From this distortion it follows that, on the chart, the shortest distance from one point to another is not always a straight line. If you link two points on the same parallel by stretching a string over a globe, then it is apparent that the string follows the arc of a great circle (a circle whose centre is the same as that of the Earth): the shortest course does not follow the parallel.

Now, on the chart, the parallels are straight lines running parallel. The navigator who wants to steer a straight line must therefore gradually change course. The straight course is called the orthodromic, or great circle course. The course by the chart is called the loxodromic, or rhumb line course. Note that there is no need to take this peculiarity into account on coastal cruises, or even on long passages when the distances are not great enough for the difference between the great circle and the rhumb line courses to make any significant difference to the distance covered.

Reading the chart

Reading charts needs practice. The information contained is often given in the form of conventional signs and abbreviations, which you must be able to decipher without making any mistakes. We will only deal with the subject briefly; the Admiralty chart 5011 (or, in France, the Guide du navigateur) will give you all the necessary information.

Scales

The northern and southern edges of a chart (north is at the top) give a longitude scale, which allows you to locate yourself in relation to the Greenwich meridian. This is rarely needed.

The western and eastern edges give the latitude scale. This allows you not only to work out the latitude, but above all to calculate distances, since one minute of latitude equals one nautical mile.

The latitude scale varies, as we know. One minute of latitude is

47

The distances are measured on the latitude scale. The distance from the Bodic light to the light at les Héaux is 6 nautical miles as the crow flies (Admiralty Chart 2668).

represented by a greater distance on the chart as we approach the poles. Even if this increase is not apparent just from looking at the chart, it must nonetheless be taken into account. In order to measure the distance between two points, the distance must be measured on the chart at the level of the mean latitude of the two points in question.

Heights and depths

The three zones on the charts are quite distinct: the sea, that is to say places where there is always water; terra firma , where there is never any water and the foreshore, which is sometimes under water and sometimes not.

On old charts, the sea is white, the land is an even grey, and the foreshore is shaded grey according to the nature of the sea bed. On new maps, which are in colour, the sea is blue where it is relatively shallow, with the colour lightening as the water deepens. From a depth of 20m, the sea is represented as white. The land is khaki, and the foreshore is grey-brown (khaki and blue super-imposed).

On all charts, the contours of the sea bed are denoted by lines referred to as depth contours, and the depth is given by soundings. The soundings are given in metres, and are based on the lowest astronomical tide (coefficient 20). This level is known as the chart datum.

There are still charts to be had in Britain that give soundings in feet and refer to the average spring tides (coefficient 95). It is therefore just as well to find out which scale is being used on the chart in question.

Drying heights are given in metres, and in relation to the same reference level. However, the height uncovered at low water is underlined on the chart. 3·5 indicates a point emerging 3·5m at low water.

Heights are also given in metres or feet, but relate to mean high

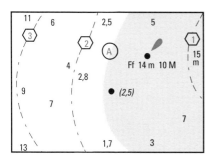

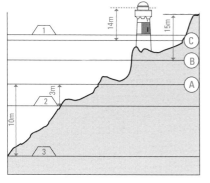

Different datum levels are used for soundings and heights.
A datum level for soundings or depths, (LAT lowest astronomical tide, coefficient 20).
B datum level for heights (level at half-tide, coefficient 70).
C datum level for height of the lights on lighthouses (MHWS mean high water spring tide, coefficient 95).
Consequently, the height of the light on the lighthouse (14m on the chart) and the height of the top of the slope do not have the same datum level as the one used for depths.

1 Highest astronomical tide level (HAT)
2 Sounding (3m depth contour)
3 Sounding (10m depth contour)

water springs, or mean sea level. In order to avoid any possible confusion with the soundings, the figures are followed by an 'm'.

On French charts rocks that are always exposed are represented by a D on recent charts, and by a T on the older charts in black and white.

The seascape

Scales and levels give the basic facts, but the chart has many other indications, which, taken together, provide a picture of the seascape that is suited to the needs of navigators. On the chart, the land looks bare, merely an area for landmarks: it consists only of high points, conspicuous buildings and the more stately trees. The world only really begins at the water's edge, with its precise boundaries. It is a curving, uneven region of blank area between particular features. The smallest buoy has the importance normally accorded to a village. The magenta marks showing lights catch the eye in just the same way as the lights do themselves at night. All in all, the seascape is most accurately portrayed by the chart.

There is only one way to learn to read a chart: look at it for a long time, and orientate it to the area it describes. We shall leave it at that. For an example, look at the chart for les Glénans, appended at the end of the book – there is plenty there to be going on with for the moment. Don't forget to look at others from time to time: a few good charts are much more entertaining than the television on winter evenings.

Keeping charts up to date

People will be glad to know that the charts produced by the SHOM are divided up into seven categories: from charts for coastal navigation (scale from 1 to 10,000 up to 1 to 25,000) right up to charts of shipping lanes and globes (scales from 1 to 5,000,000 to 1 to 15,000,000), passing through charts for seagoing, coasting, landfalls, sea crossings and maps of the oceans. Every map carries a number, which helps prevent confusion. The Admiralty catalogue of charts (NP 131) lists around six thousand charts, enough to sail safely round the world. An extract of the catalogue covering the British Isles and Western Europe (NP 109) is published in January each year.

Admiralty charts are kept scrupulously up to date. When buying a chart from a registered agent, check the delivery date (marked on the bottom of the chart) and then ask for the *Notices to Mariners* that have appeared since. These will give any necessary corrections.

My address:
The Admiralty Hydrographic Dept,
Creechbarrow, Taunton,
Somerset, TA1 2DN;
tel. 01823 337900,
fax 01823 284077.

Charts that you have had for a while can be corrected from the Admiralty's *Notices to Mariners: Small Craft Edition*, which is published every April. Corrections should be made with indelible ink, preferably magenta; the date and number of corrections made should also be marked in the left-hand margin, so that you can tell how up to date the chart is. You should try to keep all your references up to date with the relevant supplements.

Remember that when buying foreign charts it will not always be possible to keep them precisely up to date, and therefore they must be used with a great deal of care. The plastic-covered charts (coded 'p' by the SHOM) are difficult to keep up to date.

Note that in order to keep a chart reliable, it must remain perfectly legible – taking good care of it is a matter of safety.

Pilot books

Pilot books are the fruit of many centuries of experience. They are the result of observations made at every latitude, by generations of sailors. This body of information is checked and updated every day of the year, and is an irreplaceable source of information.

The Pilot books ought to be consulted at the same time as the charts: they are an important aid to understanding them properly. Originally produced for merchant ships, they inevitably see life from a more lofty perspective, which is easy to understand, given that merchant ships are a little taller. Nonetheless, information specifically targeted at the amateur sailor is beginning to appear. In any event, even the information pertaining to large vessels is useful, providing the necessary adaptations are made.

Each volume of the Pilot books is divided into two parts. The first is given over to general items of information relating to the region in question: meteorology, oceanography, geography, regulations, sea routes, landfalls. The second is a description of the coast, with its dangers, marks, buoyage (for daytime), tides, currents, channels, anchorages, ports and what they have available in the way of resources. This information is complemented by sketches and profiles of the coast.

The French Pilot books (*Instructions Nautiques*) also contain a volume of plates (charts of ports and panoramic shots of the coast).

Keeping Pilot books up to date

The procedure below describes the situation in France in detail. British publications are updated regularly in a similar manner. Every Pilot book is designated by a letter and a number. The letter indicates the series to which the Pilot book belongs, and is also keyed into the corresponding *List of Lights*. The number relates to the region described by the Pilot book. Thus, the Pilot book dealing with the northern and western coasts of France carries the reference number C2. Those Pilot books with fixed pages also carry a number giving the year of publication.

Each volume of the Pilot books purchased must be accompanied by a pamphlet of corrections (or a group of replacement pages for the volumes published in loose leaf format).

In order to keep the Pilot book up to date, get hold of the pamphlet of corrections or the replacement pages which are updated and published every year.

In addition, in order to be properly up to date, also consult the last summary table that appeared in the *Weekly Notices to Mariners* (groups 10, 20, 30 etc.), all the tables that have appeared since the publication of the last summary table, and the last list of notices that is still valid. If you do find yourself forced to sail in a boat which is

51

not equipped with properly updated chart information, extra care is advised!

Other nautical publications

There are, naturally enough, other publications in addition to the official ones. They are not intended to replace the latter, but often draw together a good deal of information, which would otherwise be spread out through a number of Admiralty publications, in a single volume. A visit to a chandler or a good specialist section in a bookshop should enable you to select one which suits your needs.

The Almanach du Marin Breton

Published by the discreet Oeuvre du Marin Breton, this almanac is extremely useful when sailing along the Channel and Atlantic coasts. It contains information on buoyage, a table of tides for certain ports, the list of lights and lighthouses from the entry to the North Sea down to Saint-Jean-de-Luz along with a very clear description, as well as advice on sailing at night in these waters. There is also a list of radio-beacons, with their characteristics, a list of sea charts, much more useful information on other subjects, and a good number of amusing anecdotes thrown in for good measure. This annual provides incomparable value for very little money, and its owner can be confident of having completely up-to-date information.

The almanac for the year in progress appears on the first of September for that year, but you can also get supplements on the first of January and the first of June.

Cruising Association Handbook

This publication gives detailed information on harbours, hazards, buoyage systems, leading lights and transits for all major and most minor anchorages likely to be of interest to the cruising sailor.

Macmillan and Silk Cut Nautical Almanac

This publication, which includes the *Yachtsman's Handbook*, provides detailed ephemeral information such as star diagrams and tables, tidal information, and selected harbour and other information. The *Handbook* contains information which is expected to change less frequently.

Yachtsman's sailing directions

Specific and authoritative *Sailing Directions* are published by the Irish Cruising Club, the Clyde Cruising Club, the Forth Yacht Clubs Association etc. A list of these can be obtained from the Royal Yachting Association, Romsey Road, Eastleigh, Hampshire, SO5 4YA, England.

Reed's Nautical Almanac

This almanac is a standard work, and gives the same sort of information not only for British waters (as far as Iceland), but also for the Dutch, Belgian and French coasts, down to Saint-Jean-de-Luz.

Much of the work is given over to navigation by the stars (and gives the appropriate tables). There is also a great deal of invaluable information concerning the tides and tidal currents in the Channel.

An update for the almanac for the year in progress is published in April.

The Admiralty pilots

These Admiralty works, along the lines of the *Instructions Nautiques*, are extremely precise and detailed. In particular, leading lines and transits are described in considerable detail, and with a good number of sketches.

Publications of interest to amateur sailors

A good deal of additional information directly targeted at amateur sailors can be found in various cruising guides and in the different sailing magazines published throughout Europe. Descriptions of the various areas in which one might be sailing can be found in the appropriate magazines for the country in question. The descriptions will usually be accompanied by photos and sketches of use to the amateur sailor.

These studies are generally put together by responsible people, but it must always be remembered that the information given concerning buoyage and lights can, as with any other yachting publication, go out of date very quickly. Consequently, while such magazines can provide a useful supplement to the information given in the more official publications, the more established works on the subject are still of central importance.

Calculating the tides

The tides are an important factor in the life of the sea, but for the present we will limit ourselves to a discussion of the means by which the sailor can take account of the tides for the purposes of navigation: publications and methods that allow one to know the depth of water underneath the keel, and practical information on tidal currents or streams.

Tide tables

Since we know the relative movements of the planets, it is quite possible to work out the movement of the tides for any given place and

These photographs of the port of Sauzon were taken six hours apart.

any given time, that is to say, the difference between the water levels at high tide and low tide respectively, along with the times at which these highs and lows will occur. The tide tables are produced every year and do not have to be kept up to date within that year.

The tide tables contain:

■ A table showing the coefficients for the different tides that year. The coefficient is a measure, used in France, indicating the amplitude of the tide. It is given in hundredths, and the coefficients used as reference points are:

C= 120 for the largest tide known (highest astronomical tide)
C= 95 for mean spring tides
C= 70 for mean tide
C= 45 for mean neap tides
C= 20 for the smallest tide known (lowest astronomical tide)

The range of the tides varies considerably from one place to another, depending on the bottom and the shape of the coastline. Consequently, on the same day (and therefore for the same coefficient) the range can be 11·2m at Saint-Malo and 4·6m at Lorient. Note, however, that in any given place, the relation between the ranges is equal to the ratio of the coefficients. Accordingly, the range at maximum spring tide is six times greater than the range at maximum neap tide (120= 6 x 20).

■ The heights at high tide and at low tide for 18 main ports, and then the corrections required to estimate the tides in 215 secondary ports to be found in Britain, France, Belgium, the Netherlands and Spain.

Figures are also given for the tidal flow, hour by hour, in the Solent and at Le Havre and Saint-Malo. In these places, the normal tidal flow is affected by local conditions. There are also graphs given for the tides in various ports, and a table of corrections to allow for the effect of atmospheric pressure on water levels.

Some comment should also be made on the hours shown and the levels at half tide.

Times
When consulting a document on tides, always check what time is being used as a reference. In the French tide tables, the time used is GMT + 1 ; an hour should be added in summer.

Heights
Heights are given in metres, in relation to the datum. However, the datum is not the same for all countries. Most countries, including France, have chosen the level of the lowest astronomical tide. This

seems to be a fairly safe principle to follow, given that, apart from in a few exceptional cases, the actual depth of the water is never less than the depth given in the tables. Sometimes, indeed, it is rather deeper: at Paimpol, for example, the datum chosen as zero on the charts is in fact 50cm above the level of the lowest astronomical tide.

However, in certain other countries, such as Britain, there are still documents that use the Mean Low Water Springs as a reference level. When you calculate the low water depth of above-average spring tides, you will have heights that will be less than the datum.

Half tide level

Note that, whatever the range is at a given spot, the level of the sea is always the same at half tide. This half tide level is given in the tide tables for each of the standard ports as well as for most of the secondary ones (it is also to be found on the label of most charts). It can also be referred to as the mean level, and is an invaluable reference, as will be seen.

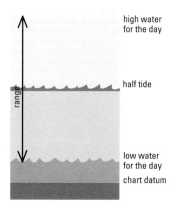

$$range = high\ tide - low\ tide$$
$$mean\ level = \frac{high\ tide + low\ tide}{2}$$

Methods of calculation

When sailing near the coast, there are various possible reasons for wanting to calculate the flow of the tides. One of the main concerns is to keep a sufficient distance between the keel and the sea bed. However, calculating the tide can also be of use in determining the appearance of the coastline you are approaching: it will tell you which rocks will be above water, and which ones will be submerged. Finally, sometimes the combined use of soundings and tidal calculations can give an idea of position – this is especially useful in very foggy conditions.

In practice, it is a matter of finding out:

■ the depth of water in a given place at a given time,
■ or the time when there will be a certain depth of water in a given place. The calculations are made on the basis of the times of high and low water. All that is needed now is the method.

The rule of twelfths

There is no lack of methods for calculating the times and the heights of the tides: there are ones for every occasion and to suit all tastes. We will keep to an explanation of the method that seems simplest, which is known as the rule of twelfths. Then we will deal with other methods which might be useful in areas where the tides show some peculiarity.

The rule of twelfths is based on a simple observation: the tidal curve is very like a sine curve. From one slack water to the next, the sea rises or descends by:

1/12 of its range in the 1st hour	1
2/12 of its range in the 2nd hour	2
3/12 of its range in the 3rd hour	3
3/12 of its range in the 4th hour	4
2/12 of its range in the 5th hour	5
1/12 of its range in the 6th hour	6

This is what is known as the rule of twelfths.

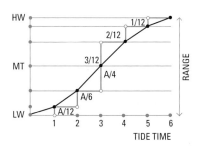

Since the range is divided by 12 and the time interval between two slack waters by 6, it is very easy to figure out the depth of water from hour to hour. Note however, that since the interval is, on average, longer than six hours, the tide time is different from clock time. Having said that, the difference does not need to be taken into account except when the time interval is very different from this average (which happens in the English Channel, for example, where time intervals can be less than 5 hours or more than 7 hours). Practically speaking, one does not need to make corrections unless the time interval is less than five and a half hours or more than six and a half hours.

Given that some navigators hate drawings, and some hate calculations, it is a happy coincidence that the rule of twelfths can be used either by calculation or graphically.

Calculation for a standard port

Supposing we are at Shoreham on 3 July, and we want to know the following things:
- ■ what will be the depth of water in the port at 1220?
- ■ at what time will the water be 4m deep?

This is an easy example, since Shoreham is one of the standard

ENGLAND, SOUTH COAST — SHOREHAM

Lat 50°50' N Long 0°15' W

TIME ZONE GMT
For Summer Time add ONE hour in non tinted area

TIMES AND HEIGHTS OF HIGH AND LOW WATERS

YEAR 1986

	MAY				JUNE				JULY				AUGUST		
	Time	m	Time	m	Time	m	Time	m	Time	m	Time	m	Time	m	Time	m

MAY

1 0358 5·1 / 1030 1·7 / Th 1656 5·1 / (2321 1·9
16 0312 4·7 / 0937 1·9 / F 1556 4·9 / 2218 2·1

2 0524 4·8 / 1157 1·8 / F 1825 5·0
17 0420 4·6 / 1044 2·0 / Sa 1712 4·8 /) 2333 2·0

3 0050 1·9 / 0656 4·6 / Sa 1321 1·7 / 1942 5·2
18 0540 4·6 / 1201 1·9 / Su 1828 5·1

4 0203 1·7 / 0810 5·0 / Su 1426 1·5 / 2040 5·5
19 0046 1·8 / 0653 4·9 / M 1312 1·6 / 1933 5·4

5 0259 1·4 / 0903 5·3 / M 1515 1·2 / 2125 5·7
20 0147 1·4 / 0754 5·3 / Tu 1411 1·2 / 2026 5·7

6 0343 1·1 / 0944 5·6 / Tu 1558 1·0 / 2204 5·9
21 0242 1·0 / 0844 5·7 / W 1504 0·9 / 2113 6·0

7 0420 0·9 / 1020 5·8 / W 1635 0·9 / 2238 5·9
22 0332 0·7 / 0932 6·0 / Th 1555 0·7 / 2200 6·3

8 0455 0·8 / 1053 5·8 / Th 1708 0·8 / ● 2309 6·0
23 0421 0·6 / 1021 6·1 / F 1644 0·6 / ○ 2247 6·4

9 0526 0·8 / 1125 5·8 / F 1740 0·8 / 2339 5·9
24 0510 0·6 / 1112 6·2 / Sa 1731 0·7 / 2334 6·4

10 0556 0·8 / 1157 5·8 / Sa 1810 1·0
25 0557 0·7 / 1205 6·3 / Su 1819 0·8

11 0006 5·8 / 0624 0·9 / Su 1229 5·7 / 1839 1·1
26 0021 6·4 / 0645 0·8 / M 1257 6·2 / 1908 1·0

12 0034 5·7 / 0654 1·0 / M 1259 5·6 / 1911 1·3
27 0108 6·2 / 0733 1·0 / Tu 1347 6·1 / 1958 1·2

13 0102 5·5 / 0725 1·2 / Tu 1333 5·4 / 1944 1·5
28 0157 6·0 / 0822 1·1 / W 1439 5·9 / 2052 1·4

14 0136 5·3 / 0801 1·5 / W 1410 5·2 / 2025 1·8
29 0249 5·6 / 0915 1·3 / Th 1535 5·6 / 2152 1·6

15 0219 5·0 / 0844 1·7 / Th 1457 5·0 / 2116 2·0
30 0349 5·3 / 1016 1·5 / F 1637 5·4 / (2259 1·7

31 0458 5·0 / 1125 1·7 / Sa 1748 5·2

JUNE

1 0012 1·8 / 0614 4·8 / Su 1236 1·7 / 1855 5·2
16 0453 4·9 / 1115 1·6 / M 1736 5·2 / 2357 1·6

2 0120 1·7 / 0723 4·9 / M 1341 1·6 / 1954 5·3
17 0601 5·0 / 1222 1·5 / Tu 1841 5·4

3 0217 1·6 / 0821 5·0 / Tu 1435 1·5 / 2044 5·4
18 0104 1·4 / 0706 5·2 / W 1330 1·3 / 1943 5·6

4 0305 1·4 / 0908 5·2 / W 1522 1·3 / 2128 5·5
19 0207 1·2 / 0807 5·4 / Th 1432 1·1 / 2040 5·8

5 0349 1·2 / 0949 5·4 / Th 1603 1·2 / 2208 5·6
20 0306 1·0 / 0906 5·7 / F 1530 0·9 / 2135 6·0

6 0426 1·1 / 1028 5·5 / F 1641 1·1 / 2242 5·7
21 0402 0·8 / 1003 5·9 / Sa 1626 0·9 / 2228 6·2

7 0502 1·0 / 1106 5·6 / Sa 1717 1·1 / ● 2316 5·7
22 0455 0·6 / 1100 6·1 / Su 1719 0·9 / ○ 2319 6·3

8 0535 1·0 / 1141 5·6 / Su 1749 1·1 / 2346 5·7
23 0547 0·7 / 1156 6·1 / M 1811 1·0

9 0606 1·1 / 1216 5·6 / M 1823 1·3
24 0010 6·2 / 0637 0·9 / Tu 1250 6·2 / 1900 1·1

10 0017 5·6 / 0638 1·3 / Tu 1250 5·6 / 1857 1·4
25 0100 6·2 / 0725 1·0 / W 1342 6·1 / 1951 1·2

11 0052 5·5 / 0715 1·3 / W 1325 5·5 / 1935 1·5
26 0148 6·0 / 0813 1·1 / Th 1429 6·0 / 2040 1·3

12 0129 5·4 / 0752 1·4 / Th 1403 5·5 / 2015 1·6
27 0237 5·8 / 0901 1·2 / F 1516 5·8 / 2131 1·4

13 0210 5·2 / 0833 1·5 / F 1445 5·4 / 2101 1·6
28 0326 5·5 / 0949 1·5 / Sa 1604 5·6 / 2220 1·6

14 0256 5·1 / 0918 1·5 / Sa 1534 5·3 / 2152 1·7
29 0420 5·2 / 1037 1·6 / Su 1658 5·4 / (2321 1·7

15 0352 5·0 / 1012 1·6 / Su 1632 5·2 /) 2250 1·7
30 0518 4·9 / 1142 1·7 / M 1757 5·1

JULY

1 0024 1·8 / 0624 4·7 / Tu 1246 1·8 / 1858 5·0
16 0513 5·0 / 1141 1·5 / W 1756 5·3

2 0127 1·9 / 0729 4·7 / W 1349 1·8 / 1958 5·0
17 0025 1·5 / 0626 5·0 / Th 1255 1·5 / 1909 5·3

3 0225 1·9 / 0829 4·8 / Th 1446 1·8 / 2052 5·1
18 0140 1·4 / 0743 5·2 / F 1410 1·4 / 2020 5·5

4 0317 1·6 / 0921 5·1 / F 1536 1·6 / 2140 5·3
19 0251 1·3 / 0854 5·5 / Sa 1519 1·2 / 2123 5·8

5 0402 1·4 / 1007 5·3 / Sa 1620 1·5 / 2223 5·4
20 0354 1·1 / 0959 5·8 / Su 1619 1·1 / 2221 6·0

6 0442 1·3 / 1050 5·5 / Su 1659 1·4 / 2300 5·6
21 0450 1·0 / 1056 6·0 / M 1714 1·1 / ○ 2313 6·2

7 0519 1·2 / 1129 5·6 / M 1734 1·4 / ● 2333 5·6
22 0541 0·9 / 1150 6·1 / Tu 1804 1·1

8 0554 1·2 / 1205 5·7 / Tu 1810 1·4
23 0002 6·2 / 0628 0·9 / W 1239 6·2 / 1851 1·1

9 0008 5·7 / 0627 1·2 / W 1240 5·7 / 1845 1·4
24 0048 6·2 / 0712 0·9 / Th 1324 6·2 / 1935 1·1

10 0042 5·7 / 0703 1·2 / Th 1316 5·8 / 1923 1·3
25 0132 6·1 / 0755 0·9 / F 1406 6·2 / 2019 1·1

11 0119 5·6 / 0742 1·2 / F 1351 5·8 / 2001 1·3
26 0213 5·8 / 0836 1·0 / Sa 1444 6·0 / 2059 1·2

12 0158 5·6 / 0820 1·1 / Sa 1429 5·8 / 2042 1·3
27 0254 5·7 / 0915 1·1 / Su 1521 5·8 / 2141 1·4

13 0238 5·5 / 0900 1·2 / Su 1509 5·7 / 2125 1·3
28 0334 5·3 / 0956 1·4 / M 1601 5·4 / 2227 1·6

14 0323 5·3 / 0944 1·2 / M 1555 5·5 /) 2215 1·4
29 0420 5·0 / 1041 1·6 / Tu 1651 5·0 / 2323 1·9

15 0412 5·2 / 1037 1·4 / Tu 1650 5·4 / 2314 1·5
30 0517 4·6 / 1138 2·1 / W 1755 4·7

31 0030 2·1 / 0632 4·5 / Th 1259 2·2 / 1908 4·6

AUGUST

1 0142 2·0 / 0749 4·5 / F 1411 2·2 / 2019 4·7
16 0126 1·7 / 0735 4·7 / Sa 1404 1·7 / 2012 5·3

2 0247 2·0 / 0856 4·8 / Sa 1511 2·0 / 2118 5·0
17 0246 1·5 / 0855 5·3 / Su 1518 1·4 / 2122 5·6

3 0340 1·7 / 0950 5·1 / Su 1600 1·7 / 2205 5·3
18 0351 1·2 / 0958 5·7 / M 1618 1·2 / 2217 5·9

4 0423 1·5 / 1034 5·4 / M 1641 1·5 / 2245 5·6
19 0444 1·0 / 1051 6·1 / Tu 1708 1·0 / ○ 2305 6·2

5 0502 1·3 / 1112 5·6 / Tu 1717 1·4 / ● 2318 5·7
20 0531 0·9 / 1137 6·3 / W 1752 1·0 / 2347 6·3

6 0536 1·2 / 1147 5·8 / W 1751 1·2 / 2351 5·8
21 0612 0·8 / 1219 6·3 / Th 1832 0·9

7 0611 1·1 / 1221 5·9 / Th 1827 1·1
22 0027 6·3 / 0651 0·8 / F 1257 6·3 / 1911 0·9

8 0025 5·9 / 0647 1·1 / F 1255 6·0 / 1904 1·0
23 0105 6·2 / 0727 0·8 / Sa 1332 6·2 / 1947 0·9

9 0102 5·9 / 0724 0·9 / Sa 1332 6·1 / 1941 0·9
24 0141 6·0 / 0801 0·9 / Su 1403 6·1 / 2021 1·0

10 0140 5·9 / 0800 0·9 / Su 1406 6·1 / 2019 0·9
25 0213 5·8 / 0834 1·1 / M 1433 5·8 / 2055 1·3

11 0216 5·8 / 0837 0·9 / M 1440 6·0 / 2058 1·0
26 0246 5·5 / 0908 1·4 / Tu 1506 5·4 / 2133 1·6

12 0255 5·6 / 0916 1·1 / Tu 1522 5·7 / 2142 1·2
27 0323 5·0 / 0950 1·8 / W 1549 5·0 / (2220 2·0

13 0337 5·3 / 1004 1·3 / W 1612 5·4 / 2240 1·5
28 0414 4·6 / 1045 2·2 / Th 1651 4·6 / 2328 2·3

14 0437 5·0 / 1109 1·6 / Th 1722 5·1 /) 2357 1·7
29 0533 4·3 / 1207 2·5 / F 1817 4·4

15 0601 4·9 / 1236 1·8 / F 1849 5·0
30 0055 2·4 / 0710 4·4 / Sa 1336 2·5 / 1946 4·5

31 0215 2·3 / 0829 4·7 / Su 1445 2·2 / 2055 4·8

Chart Datum: 3.27 metres below Ordnance Datum (Newlyn)

Reproduced from Macmillan & Silk Cut Nautical Almanac, based on British Admiralty data.

ports, and the figures for the times and levels of the tides are given in the almanac. We will come to an example of the calculations required for a secondary port later.

Let us look first of all for the times of high and low tide at Shoreham on 3 July.

| High tide | 0829 | 4.8m |
| Low tide | 1446 | 1.8m |

Here we go!

Question 1: what will be the depth of the water at 1220?

■ Given that it is summer, we will use GMT + 1 instead of GMT.
High tide   0929
Low tide   1546
■ calculation of a twelfth
range: 4·8 – 1·8= 3·0m (HW minus LW)
twelfth: 3·0/12= 0·25m (range divided by 12)
■ to calculate the time of the tide (interval divided by 6):
interval: 1546 – 0929 = 6 hours 17 mins or 377 mins
tide-hours: 6 hrs 17/ 6 = 1 hr 3 mins, or 63 minutes by the clock
■ At 1220, the tide has been going down for 2 hours 51 mins, thus 171 mins by the clock . This time must be converted into tide-minutes by using a rule of three:
(171 x 60) / 63 = 163 tide-minutes, thus 2 hr 43 mins in tide-hours)

The sea has therefore gone down by approximately 5/12, or about 1·25m. At 1220, the depth of the water at Shoreham will therefore be:
4·8 – 1·25 = 3·55m.

Question 2: at what time will the water be 4m in depth?

When the water level is at 4m, the sea will have dropped by 4·8 – 4·0 = 0·8m, ie just over 3/12.

The sea goes down by 3/12 in 2 hours, thus about 120 tide - minutes. By the rule of three, we can convert tide - minutes into clock - minutes:

(120 x 63)/60 = 126 mins, or 2 hrs 6 min
So, the water level will be 4m at:
0929 + 0206 = 1135.

The semi-circle

On a vertical scale calibrated in metres, a semi-circle is drawn with a diameter equal to the range of the tide, taking care to make low water and high water fall at the required depth. The half circum-

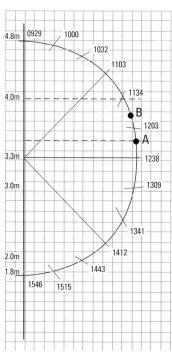

In order to divide the semi-circle into twelve, three radii are marked: one at right angles to the vertical, the others at 45°. With the compasses still adjusted to the radius of the semi-circle, you mark out the required intersections from the five radii (the last two are obtained from the intersections which are above and below the horizontal radius).

59

ference is then divided into six, or better still into twelve, equal parts, corresponding to each hour or half hour of tide. The graph should be drawn on squared paper (preferably in millimetres) if it is to be readable.

■ Depth of water at 1220: point A at 1220 on the semi-circle falls on the horizontal 3·55m.

■ The time at which there is 4m of water: the horizontal for 4m meets the semi-circle at point B, which is about 1135.

Calculations and reality

Whatever method is used to calculate the depth of the water, always remember that the results are approximate (different results can be obtained by using different methods). A variety of factors can contribute to this imprecision: atmospheric pressure for example (don't forget to consult the back page of the Tide Tables, which has a table that allows you to correct the results according to the atmospheric pressure on that day). Equally, the wind can cause variations that must be allowed for, even though there is no good way of predicting exactly how great the difference will be (it can be between +/-20cm and +/-50cm). Generally speaking, when the atmospheric pressure is high and the wind is from the land, the depth of the water will be less than the figures derived by calculation, and it will be greater when the pressure is lower and the wind is from the sea.

On the other hand, swell causes a variation in level that corresponds to half the height of the wave. If it is remembered that the swell tends to increase in shallower water, then one must always allow a certain safety margin.

All this goes to show that there is no real need to make complicated calculations. If you get seasick, then you'll only make mistakes anyway. Unless one is dealing with a particular case, then it is best to stick to an estimate somewhere around mean level. Caution counsels that this should then be increased by a margin of about 30cm, which is known as the pilot's foot.

A simple calculation from mean level

Since the mean level of the tide is constant for a given spot, it forms a very useful reference point. This mean level is always indicated in the tide tables for every port, whether standard or secondary.

According to the rule of twelfths, the sea level varies by a quarter of its range during the hour preceding half tide, and by another quarter during the hour following it. All that is needed is to calculate this quarter (in our example 3·0m/4 = 0·75m); this result then gives us two more interesting facts:

■ one hour before half tide: 3·3 + 0·75m = 4·05m
■ one hour after half tide: 3·3 − 0·75m = 2·55m

This rule of quarters seems sufficient in most cases, especially if allowance is made for the pilot's foot.

The pilot's foot

A foot on a ruler is about 30cm. In fact, it has been noted that the older a pilot gets, the more his foot grows. Experience teaches caution, especially as one grows to realise that it is altogether more pleasant to sail without having to worry, rather than to be constantly wondering whether one has allowed a sufficient margin or not. With this in mind, it does seem that the rule of quarters, plus a pilot's foot equal to half the range, ensure complete relaxation (let those who have never gone aground cast the first stones – if they dare). More exact calculations are only necessary when circumstances do not allow for such a safety margin.

In certain cases, indeed, one has to make do with very little. One can reasonably reduce the pilot's foot to about 30cm if the sea is calm, the bottom sandy and the tide rising, for example.

Take every possible opportunity to check your calculations by observation. For example, if there is a rock marked on your chart which you can see breaking surface, then this gives a precise indication of the level of the water. In addition, most ports have tide gauges.

Specific cases

Calculation for a secondary port

The example we chose to illustrate the rule of twelfths was a standard port: Shoreham. However, nobody spends all their time (thank heavens!) sailing in the immediate vicinity of a standard port: this could get rather dull after a while. Consequently, in order to calculate the tide for other areas, we must look up the tide tables, which give the range and times for the nearest secondary port.

Note that, here again, the differences are usually negligible. Do not make corrections unless there is a difference of at least 10 minutes or 0·3m between the standard and secondary ports in question.

In some areas, however, corrections do have to be made. Let us take Littlehampton as an example. Littlehampton is a secondary port where the range and hours of the tide are slightly different from those given for the nearest standard port (Shoreham).

Let's run through the same questions as we used for Shoreham:

What will be the water level at Littlehampton on 3 July at 1220?

From the tide tables we can see that different corrections must be applied depending on whether we are in the spring or neap tides. We must begin by checking the coefficient: this is currently 0·57, and so we must be in a period of neap tides. There is a 10 minute difference between high water at Littlehampton and Shoreham, and the same (in the other direction) at low water.

This allows us to make the following calculation:

HW	Shoreham	0829
Correction		+ 0010
HW	Littlehampton	0839
LW	Shoreham	1446
Correction		− 0010
LW	Littlehampton	1436

In order to be able to use this directly, we go from GMT to GMT + 1, which is the time used in summer. Therefore:

HW	Littlehampton	0939
LW	Littlehampton	1536

The same corrections apply to the depth as well, so:

HW	Shoreham	4·8m
Correction		− 0·4m
HW	Littlehampton	= 4·4m
LW	Shoreham	1·8m
Correction		− 0·2m
LW	Littlehampton	= 1·6m

All that remains to be done now is to apply the rule of twelfths. It would be good practice if you made the calculations for yourselves. The answers are at the end of the chapter.

Special tables

Certain places on the English channel have very particular tidal patterns. In France, there is the bay around Saint-Malo, and the estuary of the Seine; in England, there is the Solent, which lies between the Isle of Wight and the mainland.

■ In the tide tables, the water levels are given hour by hour for le Havre and Saint-Malo.

■ The *Table Permanente des Hauteurs d'Eau* (fascicules 530 A and 530 B for the Channel) is a very useful guide.

■ For the Solent, the necessary information is given in *Reed's Nautical Almanac*.

Tidal streams

All kinds of general and specific information on the streams can be found in the nautical almanacs and Pilots. Many charts have insets in

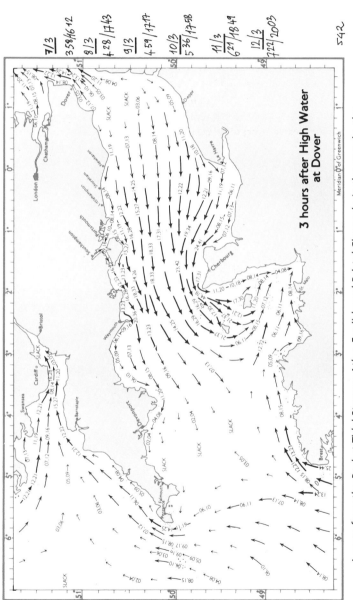

3 hours after High Water at Dover

7/3 3⁵⁸/16¹²
8/3 4²⁸/17⁴³
9/3 4⁵⁹/17⁷⁷
10/3 5³⁶/17⁵⁸
11/3 6²¹/18⁴⁹
12/3 7²²/20⁰³

542

A page from the Pocket Tidal Streams Atlas, English and Bristol Channels. In the margin, the navigator has noted the times of day when these tidal conditions will occur for the next six days.

which the speed and direction of the stream are shown, area by area and hour by hour.

However, there are also some more specialised works. For the Channel, there is the *Pocket Tidal Streams Atlas*, published by the Hydrographic Dept. This is very useful when crossing the Channel, but is less accurate for coastal areas (except for the Solent and the Channel Isles, which have special sections devoted to them). It nevertheless shows the times at which the tide turns in given areas, and this is usually enough for navigational purposes.

There are also charts of tidal streams produced by the publisher Éditions Maritimes et d'Outre-mer. These are very well produced, extremely clear and easy to read, and carry insets for particular streams around le Havre, Cherbourg and the Solent. The main problem is that the Channel is divided among three charts, which are much more expensive and much more bulky than the *Pocket Tidal Streams Atlas*.

In order to use these works properly, refer back to the almanac from time to time. This gives clear explanations of how to use the information provided. For the present, we will just note the following facts:

■ the direction of the tidal stream is the direction in which it is going, not where it is coming from (unlike wind direction);

■ the times are given by four figures next to each other, preceded by a plus or a minus sign. A plus means 'after high water', and a minus 'before high water'. For example, the almanac may give 'the stream runs WSW at about + 0430 Cherbourg', which means 4 hours 30 minutes after high water at Cherbourg;

■ speeds indicated correspond to tides of coefficient 45 or 95 (average Neap and Spring tides); from this, the speed for a given coefficient can be calculated, but in practice one can generally just take one of the two figures, depending on the day.

It must be emphasised again that the information given in these documents is approximate. It is impossible to make precise allowances for highly changeable conditions which can be influenced by a variety of factors. Moreover, the documents cannot give all details, and describe what happens in every nook and cranny of the coast: sailors must learn to figure out what is influencing the flow of tides in their own immediate vicinity.

All in all, you must develop a nose for these sorts of things. Reference marks and publications are indispensable, but they will never entirely replace the seamanship and experience that allow the sailor to adapt to local conditions and to know what is happening in a reality that has little respect for corrections and daily updates.

The answers to the tidal calculations on page 62 are: at 1220 there will be 3.35m of water; there will be 4m of water at 1105.

3

NAVIGATION
INSHORE

Right! Off we go! Now what we learned in the previous chapter can be put to practical use. Landmarks will be used as transits for navigating close to the coast. When we are a little further out, we shall take bearings to fix our position accurately on the chart. And in turn, on the chart, we shall see how to take into account factors such as the leeway and tide, and thereby how to set a course to steer by.

Pilotage, fixing one's position and choice of course are the main preoccupations of the navigator in sight of land. Further offshore, navigation is clearly a different problem.

Pilotage

In good visibility, and when there are plenty of landmarks, it is quite easy to navigate and to calculate the distance covered by what one can see. This is known as pilotage.

The essential reference works are, in the first place, the chart and, in addition, the Admiralty Pilot, tide tables and the *List of Lights*. A piece of sailmaker's thread is the only vital tool, although a bearing compass and a Cras ruler or protractor ruler can also come in handy.

Although the pilot's tools are simple, pilotage is an exacting technique, requiring method and discipline. Approximations may well be enough when you are sailing in a completely clear area where there are no immediate dangers. To this end, relative positions can give a reasonably accurate guide that is often enough. However, it is a very different matter when you approach land, enter a narrow channel or sail along a coast strewn with reefs. Trusting to flair and accuracy of vision alone becomes a dangerously hit-or-miss affair, for the simple reason that it is impossible to judge distance by eye accurately at sea. Something more than guesswork is needed. Essentially, pilotage consists in taking landmarks and making them work for you, by a simple and accurate system, the use of leading marks or transits.

Transits

When two landmarks appear to stand exactly one behind the other, then they are aligned: they form a transit. As a consequence, the observer must be on an extension of the line that links the two marks.

All you have to do is to choose good, clear transits on the chart, know where to find them in reality, and the world (well, the coast anyway) is your oyster. With a decent set of transits to point the way, you can enter the narrowest channels confidently. When you have them to port and starboard, you can steer a course through dangers.

With two transits, you can find your position very accurately, because you are at the intersection of two straight lines. By finding a transit, one can also, as we saw at the beginning of the book, observe the leeway of a boat and know what sort of headway is being made against the tide. Further, one can use one transit to find another.

In short, for the skilled pilot who can follow a chart well, each rock carries a wealth of possible projected lines which can be joined to lines taken from other rocks. Used this way, they can pilot you through the most treacherous waters and safely into harbour.

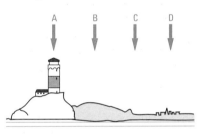

Landmarks A, C and D are good because they present a clear point or a clear vertical line. B is not a good landmark because of the rounded hilltop.

However, transit marks must be unmistakable, and for this you need good landmarks. A buoy is not a good mark, in spite of its exact outline: it moves a little in wind and tide, and that is enough to eliminate it. The same applies to a moored boat. Permanently fixed marks are needed.

Landmarks must also be as clear cut as possible: a hill without a clear top is not a good mark. Neither is a house too close to you, but its chimney might be. Lighthouses and beacons are good marks, all the more so because they are easily identifiable.

Rocks are less identifiable, but they are often all you have. Check carefully with the chart, and note their size, height and shape, which all change with the height of the tide. A rock lost among a mass of others of the same height is useless; the same goes for a rock obscured by a larger one. A very large rock, an islet or a headland can only be useful if you pick out their profiles, but remember that the tide can deceptively shorten or lengthen their slopes.

The list of possible marks is potentially endless. Generally speaking, transit marks are more precise the further apart they are and the more narrow and/or clearly defined they are.

Note that landmarks on either side of the observer can in no way be considered as transits, unless you are a seabird or some other creature with eyes on either side of your head. On the other hand, two marks slightly out of line can serve as perfectly valid transit marks on occasion. One mark is then said to be 'open' in relation to the other: rock W, for instance, open to the right of beacon X; or lighthouse Y, open two widths to the left of tower Z. This type of transit is used, either because nothing better can be found, or because there is a danger just on the transit of the two marks; all that is needed then is for the leading line to remain open for the danger to be avoided.

When a course has to be plotted in a rock-strewn area, the choice of transit marks must be carefully thought out. Although the surroundings must be used to their best advantage, they were not specifically created for that purpose. The art of pilotage is to turn even potential hazards to good use.

Open transit: the rock X is open on the right of the tower. To be more exact, we can also say that the rock is open half a width to the right of the tower.

All this requires a certain discipline. Everything must be foreseen on the chart: the course, the leading marks, the means of recognising those marks. Nothing can be left vague or obscure, and a line of reasoning must be pursued to its logical conclusion. Doubt is tantamount to error. Even if everything seems plain sailing, it is still a good idea to have alternative plans. Having said that, do not invent a variation on the spur of the moment, as this always causes problems. Finally, no daydreaming as you watch the world go by: find the marks first and admire the scenery afterwards.

While the rules of the game are simple, playing the game and thinking through moves is rather less so. Much depends on circumstance, and all the theorising in the world is probably rather less useful than one good example. The one we are going to look at concerns the Glénans islands, a region that is particularly useful for that sort of exercise.

To follow the pilot's working, you must have the same equipment as the pilot has: chart, thread and the desire to get to where you're going. In order to make things easier, we have indicated the transits and marks used on the chart of les Glénans on pages 78–9.

The ramblings of a navigator

To follow the pilot, turn to the chart on pages 78–9.

My name is Jézéquel. Suppose I'm coming from Groix and heading for Cigogne, which is one of the Glénans islands, to see Sophie, who is on a course at the famous sailing school. The wind is WSW, I don't seem to be moving terribly fast, it's getting late and I'm fed up.

The entrance

Now is not the time to get fed up. The Pilot book shows the area is littered with rocks, and there isn't much water between them. To help one move about, the Pilot points out some fine landmarks: on Penfret, a lighthouse to the north and a signal station to the south; a marker on a rock called la Pie, a 12m beacon on le Huic, and the fort and tower on Cigogne itself – no doubt with Sophie on the ramparts waiting. There is a tower beacon on Saint-Nicolas and lastly, a beacon to the SE of Bananec, on la Baleine point.

My boat draws 1m. The tide is rising: a quick calculation shows there will be about 2·5m of tide when I reach the islands.

In front of me is Penfret, easily recognised with its two hills, the lighthouse on one side and signal station on the left. Which side shall I pass? It is tempting to go in from the south: the wide Brilimec channel, with its leading mark to Cigogne, is obvious on the chart. However, to get to it, I would have to tack round some less obvious dangers lying in wait to the SE. I don't like the look of that.

Better go in from the north and pass close to Penfret; its rocky northern point, Pen-a-Men, has no foreshore.

Once past Pen-a-Men, there is a very easy entrance between Penfret and Guiriden, which looks more like a sand bank with one central rock marked (5·9m) and another marked (3·4), further to the east.

Here we go: for somebody who isn't that good at maths, it's always very annoying to see two rocks with different reference points: some related to the mean water level (figure with 'm'), and others to the lowest astronomical tide (figure underlined). All this because some always emerge and others don't. Of course, it is enough, given the half-tide level for the area, to add about 2·9m to the height given for the first rocks, to have some idea of their height relative to the others (the whole business still gets on my nerves, anyway). In short, the (5·9m) one will be much higher than the (3·4) – enough said.

Between Penfret and Guiriden is just water and one little mark, a little rocky plateau, marked (1·8) and called Tête-de-Mort. It will be covered, and I will have to steer fairly close to Penfret to avoid it.

After that, the route is clear right along to Cigogne. There is a (0·2) marked on the route, but I will have enough water to clear it.

The main problem is finding safe leading marks to get round the Tête-de-Mort rock. As I sail in I shall need a transit running roughly N–S to avoid going too far west; then an E–W line showing when I have passed the rock and can cross the first leading line.

First transit: les Méaban by Guéotec

The chart shows an entrance transit. This is splendid, but, as it is right into the wind, I can't easily use it. (I shall find out later that this transit is not easily visible from the deck of a small boat anyway.) I shall have to find an alternative. Guéotec, to the south of the channel, is surely a good landmark, as the Pilot mentions its beacon. All I need to do now is find another landmark to line up with it.

I take a piece of thread, put one end on the beacon and sweep the stretch of water between the Tête-de-Mort rock and Penfret. There is nothing suitable. Nor is there anything south of the mark and anyway

les Méaban by Guéotec

the height of the island would mean I could not see anything behind it. I may have better luck with the edges of Guéotec itself. I take my thread and pivot left and right, using the western edge as an axis: nothing to be seen. I then take the eastern edge and find something straightaway: firstly, there is a group of rocks called les Méaban with a nice little 6·5m peak, much higher than the surrounding rocks. Lining up its summit with the eastern edge of Guéotec, the thread falls bang on Tête-de-Mort. Bingo! All I need do now is keep that transit open, making sure I can always see some open water between the edge of Guéotec and the 6·5m rock, and I can avoid the rock. Excellent!

However, even if Guéotec is easy to identify, how am I going to identify my 6·5m rock? First of all, I must know in what order the rocks are going to come into view. I put one end of my thread on Pen-a-Men and sweep the channel between Guéotec and Penfret, from west to east. The first thing I find is Penfret itself. Then come the furthest rocks of the Méaban group, which are relatively low-lying (3·9 and 3·2); then there are some taller rocks (4·5m and 4·1m). In fact, it will be only when I have got away from Pen-a-Men a bit that I will be able to make out my (6·5m), which will doubtless merge with the other rocks closer up. However, if I believe my thread, there is a stretch of clear water beyond the (6.5m) mark, and then, a (3·3m), after which I will be able to see the rocks at Ruolh. So my (6·5m) rock is much higher than the others of the Méaban group, and is furthest left, with water to the left of it. This seems clear enough.

Turning right: Saint-Nicolas and la Baleine

Now I need an east-west transit so as to know when I should head straight for Cigogne after having passed the Tête-de-Mort.

Are there any good marks on the west of the islands? To the NW of Saint-Nicolas, there is the tower of le Huic. The chart says it is a former lighthouse. I like lighthouses: they are easy to see and identify. There aren't any other marks in the area, so I will try this one. With my thread on le Huic, stretching towards Tête-de-Mort, I find what I want straightaway: a (3·5m) rock at the top of the north shore of Bananec.

How am I going to identify it? I won't be able to see it when I pass Pen-a-Men, because it will be obscured by Guiriden. Will it be any clearer when I get a bit further south, and what will the seascape look like? In order to find out, I put one end of my thread on le Huic, and sweep the other end along the course I will take, following my first transit. I see that le Huic will first be obscured by Brunec, then appear to its left, and the next rock that appears will be my (3·5m). Easy!

Suddenly, I realise there has to be a much easier transit using the south coast of Saint-Nicolas and Bananec. There are some much more precise marks: the mark on la Baleine point at the end of the south–east foreshore of Bananec, and the white house on Saint-Nicolas, which must be pretty easy to spot because it is an official mark for the entry transit by the SE.

There are quite a few houses on Saint-Nicolas, but it is clear from their layout which one I want. Lining up the southernmost house on Saint-Nicolas with the mark on la Baleine is easy enough, but finding the mark is the real trick. It is yellow and black. When I reach Pen-a-Men, it will be hard to see because of the island of Drénec. The colour ought to stand out pretty well, except that the sun will be behind it and fairly low at that point.

In fact, as I go further south along my first transit, I will see it clearly in the passage between Drénec and Saint-Nicolas; it will appear to cross the passage, and when it touches the coast of Saint-Nicolas, then it will be time to go about anyway.

I have marked the transits on my chart and, because I always forget these things, I have noted in the corner my reference points, in the order they will appear: Guéotec, the (6·5m) rock from les Méaban, Drénec, Saint-Nicolas and the mark on la Baleine point.

I am now ready. Soon, the Tête-de-Mort rock will be behind me. I shall make some short tacks, not going too near Vieux-Glénan (an odd name: it can't be much older than the other islands), and finally drop anchor, in triumph, beneath the ramparts of Fort Cigogne.

Exit route

Sophie wasn't on the ramparts. She must be more interested in her bearded companions than in me. I'm off. Sitting round the fire last night under the vaults of Fort Cigogne, I heard of a little channel between le Huic and le Gluet – I'll use that on the way back. Looking for leading marks will take my mind off the fact that Sophie stood me up.

The wind is ESE this morning. The passage seems possible: I shall have the wind behind me most of the time: first to pass west of

73

Drénec, and then to move back towards le Bondiliguet. At that point, I will have to make a detour NE for a while to line myself up with the passage in front of le Huic, and the wind may be a little too much on my nose, but it seems there is room to make a short tack if necessary.

When I am ready, the tide will be low. There will be about 1m of water, so there is no question of going between Drénec and Saint-Nicolas. I will have to go round Drénec to the south.

It is quite possible to pass between Cigogne and Drénec. The (3·2) rock on the western point of la Cigogne is perfectly visible, but the (1) in the middle of the passage is less so. That (1) in the passage is in line with the (5·9m) on Guiriden and the (4·5) on la Baleine point, just to the left of the mark I used yesterday. So all I have to do to avoid the (1) is keep this transit open. What I will do is get under way and take a wide sweep to the north, as there isn't much water near Cigogne. I will draw level with the (3·2) on Cigogne, then turn slightly south.

A transit to the rear: Guéotec by la Bombe

I now need a line to go south of Drénec. There is a passage with enough water between the shore and a (2·7). I put my thread on it and straightaway find a line to the rear: the Guéotec beacon by la Bombe.

Obviously, it is not very easy to follow a line to the rear, but when piloting it is often the best solution, for the simple reason that one generally knows the leading marks behind better than the ones ahead. I know the Guéotec beacon now, and I saw la Bombe yesterday when I arrived. I can see it quite easily from where I am anchored: it is an isolated rock, and will be easy to find on the other side of Cigogne.

I always use a long enough piece of thread to find lines, and today I am glad I do: stretching my thread from the Guéotec beacon to the western edge of my chart, I note that my transit from Guéotec by la Bombe has another advantage: it allows me to pass directly out of the islands if I am unable to find leading marks to take me up to le Huic (you never know, and anyway I slept badly). There is just one rather annoying little (1·2) in the way, to the south of the tower on le Broc'h. To avoid it, I will have to change my line slightly as I pass to the south of Drénec. This will be relatively simple: I line up the Guéotec beacon with the northern edge of la Bombe instead of with the summit. After that, everything will be hunky-dory.

Rounding the coast of Drénec

I now need a line so that I can turn north after having rounded Drénec. Among the rocks on the chart, le Gluet seems to offer possibilities: there is a (9·2m) to the north, right behind a vast (9m). It ought to be fairly easy to spot two rocks in line. I find a line very quickly: le Gluet by the (5·3m) of le Bondiliguet, but spotting it in reality will be another story.

What do I see as soon as I round Drénec? I place one end of my thread on its western edge, and sweep round from west to north. There appear in turn the tower on le Broc'h (the only one in the area), then a line of large rocks: Castel Braz, Carrec Christophe, Castel Bihan. Castel Bihan ought to be easy to recognise, since it appears to be two sheer rocks (7·5m) and (7·2m) with a wide channel just to the right.

From there on, things get rather tricky. There are rocks everywhere: in the distance, le Run, le Gluet, le Huic; rather nearer the rocks on le

Bondiliguet. It will be difficult to figure out what I am looking at.

Thinking about it, it seems best to sweep the thread back in the other direction from le Huic, whose tower is easy to identify. Keeping one end of the thread on the western edge of Drénec, I put the other end on le Huic, and sweep west. I ought to see the following things:

- the (3·8m) of le Huic
- the (3·7m) on the western foreshore of Saint-Nicolas
- then, straight afterwards, the (6·4m) of le Bondiliguet
- then the various rocks of le Gluet.

The first rock to the left of le Gluet is the (5·3m) on le Bondiliguet. So when I come round to Drénec and see the tower on le Huic to the north, the (5·3m) will be just to the left of le Gluet.

That is still quite a lot to think about all at once. I will have to be on my toes when I come round Drénec. Better take some precautions: I measure the distance on the chart between the transit using le Huic and the western edge of Drénec, and the other (Gluet and the (5·3m) on le Bondiliguet): it's 200m. With a good following breeze, I will make at least 5–6 knots. Roughly speaking, I should cross the 200m in a minute. If after a minute and a half I haven't found anything, I will have to go back. Besides, I have a final mark – Job rock, a single rock ahead of me, and easy to identify, even from a distance.

A little breathing space…

All this is not quite clear. I think I'd better allow myself a little space to manoeuvre to the SW of Drénec, so I can circle around until I have found the marks I am looking for. This turning space can be easily marked out by three transit marks, two of them already known:

■ Guéotec by la Bombe, which protects me to the north;

■ le Huic by the W edge of Drénec, which protects me to the east;

■ finally, le Broc'h by Job, which completes the triangle nicely.

I shall therefore be able to circle as long as I like, and so will have plenty of time to spot the (5·3m) on le Bondiliguet. I will then follow the leading line from Gluet to the (5·3m), almost up to the rock itself.

At that point, I will have to turn to avoid the (6·4m) of le Bondiliguet, which stands between me and the exit route. Looking at the chart, it seems absurd to want a transit to make a little turn like that, but that's the sort of thinking that lost me my last boat, the Sophie VII. In any event, I have to tack to make that turn, and I could quite easily be caught out if I try it without having any leading marks.

Another exit channel

I note in passing that I can run clear out to the west if I've really had enough. To do this, I leave the Broc'h to my left, and use the des Bluiniers channel. But, just for the hell of it, I'll stick to my original plan.

Le Buquet

I place my thread between le Bondiliguet and Roc'h ar C'haor roughly along a SW–NE axis. The northern edge of Brunec or, more exactly, of le Buquet just behind it, appears between two adjacent rocks – a (7·4m) and an (8·7m). They should be easily visible, being high and rather narrow.

If I need to tack a little, I can use this gap between the two rocks as a reference point: the northern edge of le Buquet, just visible to the right of the (7·4m) will mark my northern limit, and the same edge – this time, hidden by the (8·7m) – will form my southern limit.

How am I going to recognise all this? Roc'h ar C'haor must be visible immediately on passing the transit line of le Huic by the western edge of Drénec – it's the first rock of any size to the right of le Huic.

Then, as I follow the leading line between le Gluet and the (5·3m) on le Bondiliguet, I will have to watch the scenery to my right. After Drénec, I should see Cigogne and then the signalling station on Penfret. At that moment, the two rocks that previously framed Buquet will be hidden by Roc'h ar C'haor only to reappear a moment later, and then, in the distance to the right, the island of Brunec – no problem!

The exit channel

I need a last N–S line to get me through the channel between le Huic and le Gluet, since the foreshore of le Gluet stretches out quite a way to the east. To find something that will be of use, I am forced to look a long way off: to the south of Drénec, there is the large (6·6m) rock of Fournou Loc'h. There are other rocks around it, but it lies furthest to the west and is clearly the largest.

Although the (6·6m), visible between the W edge of Drénec and the E edge of the (8m) on Quigénec, is perfect, it is quite far away, and I will have to pick it up early as I pass south of Drénec. In fact, I notice I must be heading for Fournou Loc'h as I go south between Cigogne and Drénec. It's the group of rocks just to the right of le Loch, and the (6·6m) is the rock furthest to the right. Later, when I am nearer the exit, I will see the other rocks of Fournou Loc'h disappear one by one behind the W edge of Drénec, leaving the (6·6m) alone between Drénec and Quigénec. If I miss it – which won't be too bad, I've some water to play with – then the line between the E edge of Quigénec and the W edge of Drénec will tell me. All I shall need to do is to bear away for it to reappear.

Now, I need to note down my leading marks in order.

At anchor:	(<u>4·5</u>) rock on Bananec
	(5·9m) Guiriden
	La Bombe
Going south:	(6·6m) of Fournou Loc'h
On the line Guéotec–la Bombe:	Job rock
	The tower of le Broc'h
	The tower of le Huic
	Le Gluet (4th from le Huic)
	(5·3m) on le Bondiliguet
	Roc'h ar C'haor
On the line le Gluet–le Bondiliguet:	Signal station on Penfret
	(7·4m) and (8·7m) in front
	of Brunec and le Buquet
On the line Buquet–(7·4m) and (8·7m)	Fournou Loc'h

Epilogue

I have now returned home. The scenery was quite extraordinary, which is not easy to see from my sketches, unfortunately. At all events, the sketches cannot put over the joy and pleasure one gets from identifying a rock in the midst of a group, and then being able to put a name to it. It's like being at home all of a sudden.

Whether Sophie is there or not, I'll go back to the Glénans islands and do the trip in reverse, using the passage by le Huic. All I have to do is line up Fournou Loc'h between Drénec and Quigénec: it's like fitting a key in a lock and you're at home. It's fun to work all this out. But it's time to let you get on to the next section, dear reader.

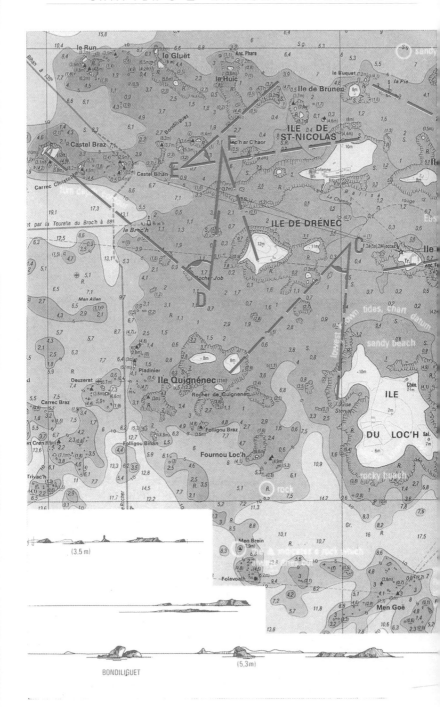

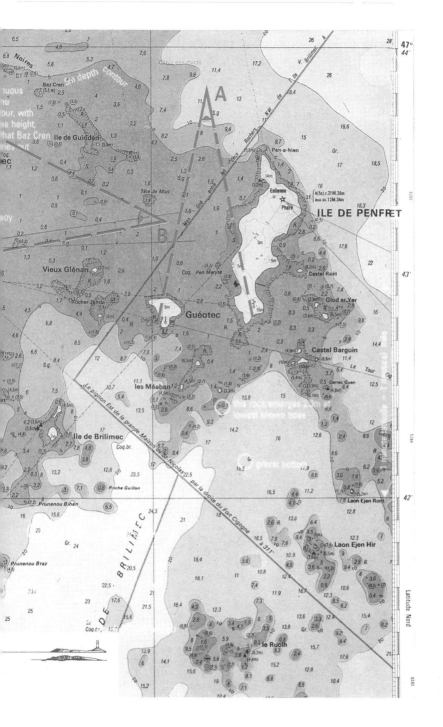

Taking a fix

A little way out from the coast, most landmarks become indistinct against the background. Soon all that remains are a few outstanding points, scattered along the horizon. Transits become scarce, and there is little likelihood of finding two at the same time to check the course.

If there are no transits then the logical thing is to navigate by bearings. The pilot's thread is replaced by more complicated equipment: the hand-bearing compass and the protractor-ruler. Arithmetic is replaced by geometry, and we move on to the serious business of taking a fix.

Taking a fix by bearings

Fixing a position means:
- taking bearings;
- correcting them for magnetic deviation;
- plotting them on the chart;
- evaluating the result.

Taking a bearing

Taking the bearing of a landmark means measuring the angle at which one sees it in relation to a point of reference (ie north).

Measurements are made with a hand-bearing compass which has a sight and a prism. A sight is taken on the mark, and the bearing shown on the compass card is read through the prism. Note that this measurement is not very accurate, especially when taken from the deck of a small boat. The further off the mark and the rougher the sea, the greater the potential for error; allow for +/-1° in flat calm, +/-2° in normal weather, and +/-5° at least in heavy weather.

In order to reduce this margin of error, it is a good idea to practise using the compass. The main thing is not to tire yourself unnecessarily: if you bring the sight up to your eye first and then sweep the horizon to find a landmark, you will only make your arms ache.

It is much easier to work in the following order: find the landmark, raise the compass to the chin and wait for it to settle, bring the sight up to your eye and then read off the bearing from the card. Take care to stand where the compass will not be deviated by metallic objects. We shall come back to this later when dealing with the ship's compass.

Correcting the bearing

The compass shows magnetic north, and we all know that this is not the same as true north (direction of the meridians). Before plotting a bearing on the chart, we must first take into account the variation, that is to say the angle between magnetic and true north. This angle varies not only according to where you are, but also varies over time and changes very slightly from year to year.

Depending on one's position, the variation can either be east or west. It is marked on the chart along with the annual increase or decrease. In the area of les Glénans, for instance, the variation was 7° 30'W in 1975; shifting by 5' E per year, it reached 6° 55'W in 1982, and is continuing to decrease.

When the variation is to the east, it must be added to the bearing shown by the compass. When it is to the west, it must be subtracted. In so doing, we convert from magnetic to true bearings.

To remember how to make the correction, the mathematically-minded will recall the formula:

True = Magnetic + Variation
Variation positive if it is east
Variation negative if it is west

The less mathematically-minded may prefer the following lines of doggerel:

Variation east, Compass Least
Variation west, Compass Best

The purists can always reproduce the little sketch in the margin from first principles.

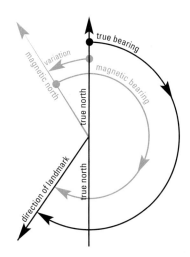

When the variation is to the west, the true bearing is smaller than the magnetic bearing.

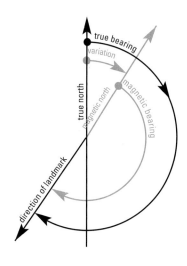

When the variation is to the east, the true bearing is greater than the magnetic bearing.

At all events, it is a good idea to find some way of remembering how the correction is to be applied without having to think too long about it. Things that seem obvious in an armchair are less so when the boat is pitching in a rough sea and you are beginning to feel thoroughly seasick.

Plotting the bearing on the chart

In order to plot the bearing on the chart, you will need a protractor to transfer the angle from the meridian or parallel, and a ruler to draw the line. Since using both instruments at once is not exactly convenient, some clever designers have come up with a contraption that combines both functions. In France, the types of protractor-ruler used most commonly are the Autocap, the Breton protractor and the Cras protractor, named after its inventor, Admiral Jean Cras.

On the Cras ruler there are two protractors, each with a double scale, and this allows you to measure an angle both from a parallel and a meridian. An arrow indicates the direction in which the rule must be set, and that's it.

The extreme simplicity of the instrument is rather startling first of all, particularly for those not exactly enamoured of figures. However, as you move the ruler over the chart, the princi-

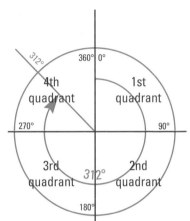

The four quadrants.

ple will quickly become apparent. To plot a bearing, you proceed by stages:

■ Place the chart as straight as possible in front of you, north to the top.

■ Place the ruler on the chart, so that its arrow points roughly in the direction of the mark that you have taken. This assumes that you know in which quadrant the mark is: for instance, a mark on a bearing of 312 is in the 4th quadrant.

■ Put one of the edges of the ruler on the mark. The easiest way to do this is to put a pencil point on the mark, and push the ruler up against it.

■ Slide and pivot the ruler so that you have at the same time:

– the most southerly centre of the protractor (this is marked with a small circle) on either a meridian or a parallel;

– on the same meridian or on the same parallel, the graduation corresponding to the bearing taken.

There is no need to twist your neck round to read this scale: the upright figures are the ones you want. Note that, of the two scales on each protractor, it is the one on the outside that applies when you are using a meridian, and the inner one when you are using a parallel.

The only problem is to be able to place the ruler exactly in relation to these three reference points: the mark, the meridian (or the paral-

Checking the hand-bearing compass: deviation

In an ideal world, the hand-bearing compass ought to indicate magnetic north. Unfortunately, however, it is subject to numerous unwelcome influences: electronics, loudspeakers, watches, the spectacle frames of the person using it, and so on, all of which can produce irregularities in the readings obtained.

If your hand-bearing compass is not reading true when you use it, your bearings can be a long way out. You therefore need to find a spot on the boat where it does not deviate.

You should periodically check that nothing has changed, by checking the hand-bearing compass against the boat's compass (and if they do not agree, finding out which is right). You can also check by measuring the bearing to a point of which you know the true bearing.

If your bearing compass is fixed to the boat it may be adjusted in the normal way.

lel), and the figures.

When the boat is heaving about, this can be something of an acrobatic feat. However, once you have managed it, all that you have to do is to make a mark (or draw a straight line if you prefer) running from the mark to where you are relative to it. You now have a position line and know that the boat is somewhere along that line, or near enough.

A two-point fix

Naturally, it takes at least two bearings to make a fix. For the best results, it is important that the two marks should not be too close together. The ideal is to have two bearings at right angles to each other. On the drawing, you can see that inaccuracy in the bearings used gives rise to a quadrilateral of uncertainty, which grows as the marks are further away, if the boat is pitching or if the navigator is tired.

A three-point fix

A fix with only two bearings is seldom accurate. It is usually necessary to take three bearings to hope for any degree of accuracy. Ideally, these marks should be about 60° apart.

Since the task can take a certain amount of time (and since the boat is still moving), it is a good idea to take the first reading on the mark that appears to be moving the least, which will be the one that is furthest away, or which lies nearest to the axis along which the boat is travelling.

When you plot these bearings on the chart, you get a triangle – a

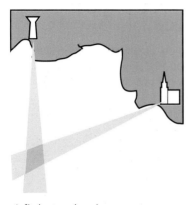

A fix by two bearings.

cocked hat.

The boat should lie within this triangle. The size of the triangle gives an initial indication of how good the fix is. If the hat is huge, then there is an error somewhere, either in the identification of the landmarks, or in the bearings themselves. If it is small, then one may assume that no glaring mistakes have been made, but remember that it is still only an approximation. If there is no hat at all, that is to say that the three bearings meet on the same point, then don't get carried away: there's probably an error somewhere. Taking a fourth bearing will show how accurate you really were.

A fix by two bearings and a transit

Sometimes one comes across a transit. The moment that one crosses that line is a good one to take a fix: all you need to do is to take two bearings, and you get not merely a cocked hat, but rather a segment bounded by the two bearings on the transit. This sort of fix is much more precise.

Checking the fix

When you have plotted the bearings on the chart and have not got too ridiculous a cocked hat for your pains, you must next check the fix and, if possible, try and improve on it. This is done by checking the chart against the scenery around you. Starting from your fix, the most obvious features should all then lie on the same bearing from you as they do on the chart.

As we are passing within sight of Trévignon point, we can use it

---

HOW TO USE THE CRAS PROTRACTOR
(opposite page)
A navigator, sailing in the vicinity of the Cap de la Hague, takes a bearing on the Basse Bréfort buoy at 213° T and wants to plot it on the chart.
• They place the protractor on the chart so that the arrow points in the direction of the bearing taken. The 213° bearing lies in the 3rd quadrant.
• They next bring the edge of the rule on to the mark and try to make the southerly centre-point of the protractor coincide with a meridian or a parallel. In this instance, it is a parallel (the bearing must therefore be read on the inner scale). The protractor is now in place: the arrow (1) is pointing in the direction of the mark; the southerly centre-point (2) is on the parallel; the bearing 213 (3) is on the same parallel. All that has to be done to plot the bearing is to draw a line starting from the mark. The boat is somewhere along this line.
(Charts by the SHOM)

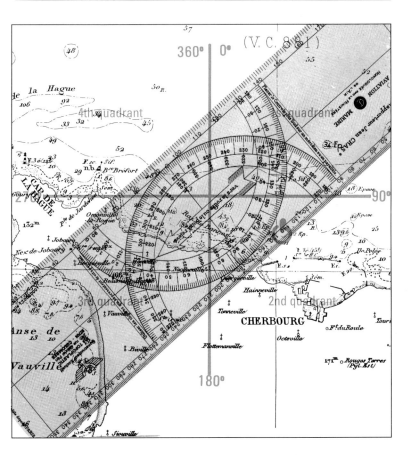

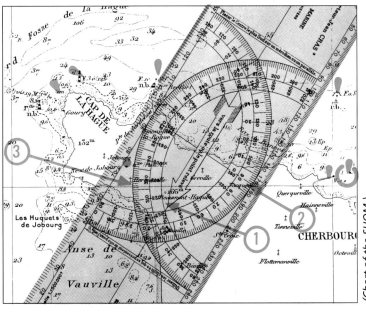

(Chart of the SHOM.)

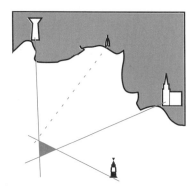

Nothing proves we are in the cocked hat. A check with a fourth bearing, however, is pretty convincing. The most precise bearing is the one taken on the closest mark (in this case the tower).

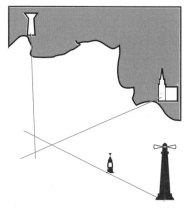

Two bearings and a transit. The transit is precise: only the bearings have any margin of error.

as an example.

The weather is good, there are marks close at hand, and in exactly the right sort of position: on the left is the beacon on les Soldats, in the middle the Trévignon lighthouse and on the right, the tower of Men-Du.

We take the following bearings:

■ les Soldats at 342°
■ the lighthouse at 19°
■ Men-Du at 69°

The corrections for variation must be included as shown on the chart: 7° 30′W in 1975, which gives – with the annual shift of 5′E – 7° 05′W in 1980 (about 7°, for the purposes of calculation).

This gives us:

■ les Soldats at 335°
■ the lighthouse at 12°
■ Men-Du at 62°

The three bearings give a decent enough cocked hat, and we must now see if the cap fits. Orientating the chart, we see that it corresponds largely to what we see: the château of Trévignon is to the right of the lighthouse; the tower of Men-Du is to the left of Raguénès; the Corn-Vas buoy is to the right of Île Verte.

Since Men-Du is the nearest mark, its bearing is probably the most precise of the three, and therefore it is likely that we are in the northern part of the hat. However, we can improve on this by tracing the angle of uncertainty of each bearing on the chart. For the current weather conditions, this is probably 2° either side of the bearings we have (see above, Taking a Bearing).

In practice there is no need to be so precise, but if the possibility of inaccuracy is not eliminated, we could equally be to either side. A mistake is easily made: supposing the bearing of Men-Du had read 59° (therefore 52° T) on the compass, instead of 69°; then the hat would have looked quite different: rather smaller, it is true, but this would not necessarily be a good sign.

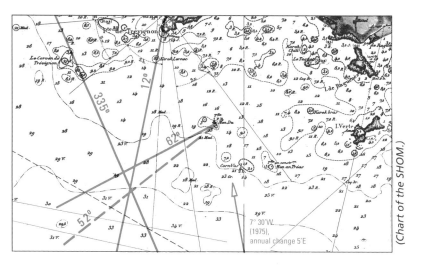

(Chart of the SHOM.)

Nonetheless, the château is definitely to the right of the light-house, and Men-Du is to the left of Raguénès. There is only one detail that would allow us to spot the error: on the chart, Corn-Vas almost forms a line with Île Verte, whereas in reality it is definitely to the right. At this point, you ought to begin to smell a rat.

Finding new landmarks

However good they may be, all landmarks have one important defect: it doesn't take long before you can't see them any more. The boat moves on, and new landmarks must always be found to form the next links in the chain. When navigating in unfamiliar waters – which is useful practice, and everyone ought to try it – finding them can be quite hard work and takes a bit of thought.

It is a good principle always to check the identity of a new land-mark against the chart, even if you think you recognise it. One of the commonest mistakes is to look at the chart for too long.

When you have identified two or three landmarks and you take a bearing on them to make a fix, it is a good idea to take a bearing on one or two marks ahead that you have not yet identified. Then plot these new bearings on the chart and see what they correspond to.

The problem can also work the other way round: you notice a useful landmark on the chart, but it is as yet impossible to pick it out. Measure the bearing on the map, and then, on deck, look for the mark with the compass. However, take care, when taking the bear-ing from the chart (which is true) and converting it into a compass bearing, that you make the required correction in the other direction. In Brittany, where the variation is west, the degree of variation must be added to the true bearing.

Where the magnetic variation remains west, the important things

87

to remember when making corrections are:

■ when bringing the compass bearing down on the chart, to subtract the amount of variation;

■ when bringing the chart bearing up to the compass, to add the amount of variation.

So: to go down, subtract; to go up, add.

No matter how careful you are, you can never be sure of not making some sort of glaring mistake. In this, as ever, common sense rules. A good method of avoiding gross errors is to check course and distance made good. If the fix shows that you have travelled 32 nautical miles in an hour, then something is not quite right (unless you've bought the wrong sort of boat). The same applies if the fix says that you have 15° of leeway to windward.

Anything that seems unlikely is probably wrong.

Using the sextant in coastal navigation

The structure is completely visible, and the height is known: this is the simplest example.

The water is visible at the base of a structure of known height: the state of the tide must be taken into account.

The base of the structure is over the horizon: both the tide and the curvature of the Earth must be taken into account.

The method of taking a fix by three bearings, described above, is the most common way of fixing position. Now, if there is a sextant on board, and you are just itching to try using it, then you will doubtless be delighted to learn that it is quite possible to use it to make a fix when navigating in sight of the coast. The sextant can even be of considerable use when you have only one mark, or when the marks are too close to one another to allow you to take a precise bearing in any other way. Moreover, there is no need to get a very expensive one – one of the plastic models will do perfectly well.

The great advantage of a sextant when compared with a compass, whose rose is never perfectly still, is that it gives a precise and definitive measurement the moment that you can line up the two points that you are trying to use.

Fix by bearing and height

Thanks to the sextant, it is possible to work out your position in relation to one landmark if its height is known. There are many landmarks whose heights can be found in the various publications, whether it is a mountain or a lighthouse. In general, lighthouses are the most common points of reference, given that their heights can be found in the *List of Lights*.

The principle is as follows: first take a bearing on the landmark, which allows you to trace a line on the chart. Then, using the sextant, measure the angle *a* between the base and the summit of the mark. Having done this, you can work out immediately how far away the mark is, and therefore the position of the boat on the line. This can be done by applying the following (simplified) formula (maximum error 10%):

$$d = (2H) / a$$

where d is the distance in nautical miles, H is the height of the mark in metres, and *a* is the angle in minutes of arc.

Some special cases apply:

■ the structure is completely visible (for example, a lighthouse) and you know the height. This is easy enough: all you have to do is make sure that the top and the base of the structure are both visible through the lens to the angle *a*.

■ the base of the mark is not visible, and the height is only given in relation to a datum – for example, coefficient 70 (half-tide level) for a hill or a mountain, coefficient 95 (mean high water springs) for the top of a lighthouse. In this case, you must first calculate the tide to be able to correct the height of the mark, allowing for the tide. Having done this, you line up both the edge of the water and the top of the mark in the lens; this will give you the angle *a*.

■ the foot of the mark is over the horizon. This is quite common since, for an observer at an altitude of 2m, the horizon is only 3 nautical miles away. This time not only does the tide have to be taken into account, but also the curvature of the Earth. This can only be done by means of a very complicated formula, so complicated, in fact, that it is usually best to use the relevant tables.

We are approaching Jersey from the SW, and we can only see that lighthouse at la Corbière. We take a bearing on it of 12°. Glancing at the *List of Lights*, we see that la Corbière is a white tower, 19m in height. The angle measured by the sextant is 7·3'.

We apply the formula: d = (2 x 19) / 7·3 = 5.2 nautical miles.

If our angle is correct, we are 5·2 miles from the light. Note that angles of less than 5' are not usable for this purpose, as the error could be greater than the angle!

Fix using horizontal sextant angles (position circles)

Taking a fix by horizontal sextant angles is useful when you have three marks which are separated by only a small angle (ie they are too close to one another).

It is known (or it is about to be known) that the geometrical position from which one can see two points, A and B, at an angle *a*, is along the arc of a circle passing through A and B. In plain English, this means that, having taken the angle subtended by A and B at the observer, it is possible to construct a circle passing through these two marks, and one can then be certain of being on that circle.

Taking in the same way the angle subtended by B and that of another landmark C, a second circle can be constructed, passing through B and C. This circle cuts the previous one at the position of the observer. Smart, eh?

To the SW of Jersey, now that the visibility is a little better, we can take a fix using this method, using three marks not too far from one another: A, the lighthouse on Noirmont point; B, the Corbière light-

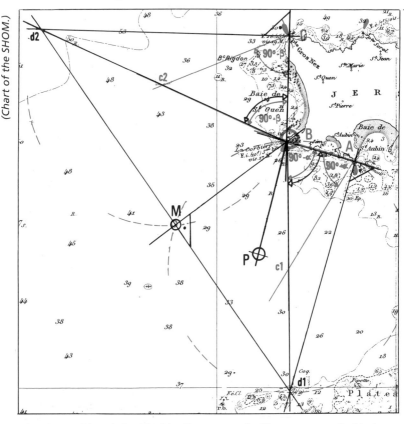

(Chart of the SHOM.)

Fix using position circles. The blue lines are marked by compasses, the black lines using a square. At P we have the fix, bearing 12° and distance 5·18 nautical miles. (Chart by the SHOM.)

house; C, the lighthouse on Gros-Nez point (on closer examination, it is apparent that we can't see it. Still, there's no holding us back on account of something like that: we can use the edge of Gros-Nez point as C).

This time the sextant must be used flat so that the images of the two marks coincide.

■ The angle between A and B is measured by the sextant: 17° (angle a) and then the angle between B and C: 22° (angle b).

■ A straight line is drawn joining A and B.

■ From A, another straight line is drawn, at an angle of (90° – a) to the line AB.

■ The same thing is done at point B.

■ The intersection of the lines is the centre c_1 of the circle, whose arc passes through both A and B.

■ The same procedure is used for B and C, in order to obtain the centre c_2 of the circle, whose arc passes through B and C.

■ The two circles intersect at M: this is the position of the boat.

If you don't have a pair of compasses, or if the arcs that have to be drawn are too large for the compasses you have, then you can use the following method:

draw a line making an angle of (90° – a) with AB through the point B.

draw a line perpendicular to AB running through A.

the two lines intersect at a point d_1.

similarly, draw a line through B at an angle of (90° – b) to BC, and then trace a line perpendicular to BC, passing through C. This gives a point d_2.

draw a straight line linking d_1 and d_2.

the line perpendicular to the segment d_1d_2, passing through B, gives the position of the boat (M).

All this routine takes a little while, as you will appreciate. To get quick at it, you need to have practised on the occasional winter evening. Navigation is an endurance sport.

Any attempt to use position circles if the sea is rough or the navigator insufficiently hardened will cause seasickness. This method is best used in calm water or at anchor, or for checking out compass deviation.

Giving a course to the helm

Steering by sight, laying course for an objective you can see, is all very well and good, but you can't always do it. There aren't necessarily any reference points visible or the visibility can be poor, and drift due to wind or current may have to be taken into account. In such cases, you have to follow a compass course. In order to give the

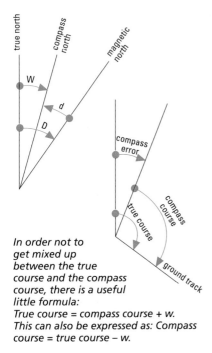

In order not to get mixed up between the true course and the compass course, there is a useful little formula:
True course = compass course + w.
This can also be expressed as: Compass course = true course – w.

helm a course to steer, the navigator must change the true course measured on the chart to a compass course in two stages:

■ Measure the true course. This can be done quite easily in the following manner: place a ruler on the course to be followed, and then slide the Cras ruler along this ruler until you make the most southerly centre of the protractor coincide with either a meridian or with a parallel. The true bearing can be read against the meridian or parallel chosen.

■ Convert the true course into a compass course. For this, you have to take into account both the magnetic variation and the compass deviation. In order to find out the value of the deviation, the instrument must be 'swung'. The sum of the variation and the deviation gives the compass error (represented by the letter w). If the compass error is to the east, it is subtracted from the true heading, and if it is west, it is added.

Giving a heading to the helm is therefore fairly simple, at least when that heading takes you directly to where you are going, and neither tidal stream nor leeway have to be taken into account. However, this is relatively rare: as soon as the wind is no longer aft, the boat will make leeway. If there is a tide running, then that's an entirely different matter. It is necessary therefore to be able to estimate the influence of these elements and take account of them when calculating the heading.

Estimating leeway and tidal stream

Estimating leeway comes with experience and familiarity with your boat. You have to watch out for it, and note how it varies according to different speeds, different sail combinations and the strength of the wind. Near to land, there will be no lack of opportunity to calculate leeway precisely. If you are passing very close to a buoy, for instance, keep an eye glued on its bearing in relation to your course away from it. At the end of ten minutes or so, take a bearing on the buoy: comparing the compass course and the compass bearing taken will give you an idea of the degree of leeway. Another way is to make a fix, then follow a precise heading, make another fix a little while later and then measure the angle of leeway on the chart.

Estimating the stream is usually more difficult. Here, it is the sea that is moving in one direction or another, taking with it everything that isn't anchored to the bottom. All you can do in this case is to trust the tidal information given in the tide tables and on the charts, which, if local conditions make it necessary, give the strength and direction of the stream hour by hour, along with the tidal coefficient. If it is stated that, for instance, between 6 and 5 hours before high water, the stream is 1·5 knots, bearing 306°, then you must take into account the fact that, whatever the heading of the boat, it will be carried 1·5 nautical miles along a bearing of 306° during the hour in question.

This is the distinction that has to be made between course through the water and course made good over the ground. The course made good over the ground, the only one that counts at the end of the day, equals the course made by the boat (as measured by the log) plus the course made by the sea in the same period. The course made good over the ground can differ wildly from the course through the water in the same period. Laying a course in such circumstances can be a very tricky operation.

■

Swinging the compass

Choosing the right position on board and making proper compensation is usually enough to eliminate all compass deviation, at least on wooden, plastic and aluminium boats. If there is still some deviation, then the amount of that deviation must be found by swinging the compass.

The most simple way of doing this is to compare the ship's compass with the hand-bearing compass. This check should be made daily, when out of sight of land, and it is also advisable, strictly speaking, to make a check on every change of course.

For a more exact check, the boat must be anchored at a precise spot (preferably at the intersection of two transits), with landmarks all around. The boat is turned by oar, and the heading noted every time a landmark whose bearing can be measured on the chart lies on the boat's axis (either ahead or astern). Comparing the chart and compass bearings gives the variation, from which the deviation can easily be deduced. This check should also be made every time one is sailing along leading marks. If this adjustment is to be valid, then all metal objects must first be removed (for good) from the compass area. Nothing must be overlooked – especially anything made of tin, pocket knives, photo-electric cells, transistor radios and loud hailers. Don't forget to look under the cockpit floor, which is a dumping ground for a lot of objects that might cause interference.

The following examples show the kind of difficulties facing the navigator sailing around the coast of northern Brittany, focusing particularly on the stretch between the NW buoy of les Minquiers and the lighthouse at le Grand-Léjon.

First passage: no leeway

On this day, the wind is N. The boat will therefore be on a broad reach on the starboard tack. Because of the wind, there is no problem with leeway. We are in the period of the neap tides (coefficient 25), and so the current is negligible.

The bearing on the chart is 224°. Our navigator adds the magnetic variation of 7° W. The compass is properly compensated. The compass course is therefore: 224° + 7° = 231°.

Second passage: with leeway

This time the wind is WNW. The trip will therefore be a close fetch on the starboard tack. On this point of sailing, the boat will make

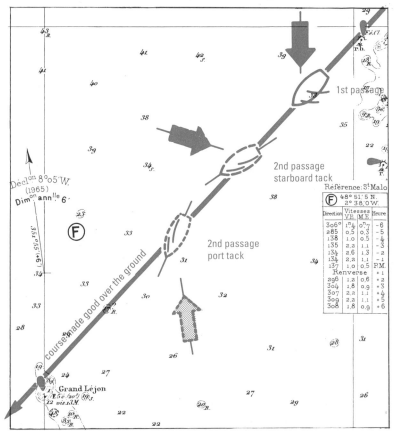

Heading of the boat (water track) in relation to the true course (ground track), with leeway made due to the wind. (Chart of the SHOM.)

considerable leeway. The navigator, who knows the boat, estimates this to be 5°, to port naturally. To arrive bang on at le Grand-Léjon, he must therefore aim 5° further to starboard, that is add 5° to the course. The calculation then is:

True course	224°
Correction for variation	+ 7°
Correction for leeway	+ 5°
Compass course	= 236°

If the wind were from the SSE, the boat would be close fetching on the port tack, and would therefore have 5° leeway to starboard. In this case, you would have to aim 5° extra to the left, that is to say to subtract 5° from the bearing. Thus:

True course	224°
Correction for variation	+ 7°
Correction for leeway	− 5°
Compass course	= 226°

If the wind were SSW, then you would have to beat. In that case, there is no point giving a course to the helm. It might even be a good idea to cover up the compass: the helm should not try to follow a course, but rather simply concentrate on making the best possible course to windward. Apart from that, the navigator should lift the corner of the veil from time to time, to see what is happening.

Third passage: with constant tidal stream

The wind is weak NE and the tides are neap. We are leaving the NW buoy of les Minquiers three hours after high water (HW + 3).

The first thing to work out is the speed of the boat. This can only really be an estimate and our navigator thinks it will be 5 knots. Since we have 19·5 nautical miles to cover, the passage will take about four hours.

In area F, during the four hours following HW + 3, the chart inset indicates the direction of the current as varying between 304° and 309°, and its speed between 1·8 and 2·2 knots at springs, 0·9 and 1·1 knots at neaps. As we are now at medium tides, we can reckon on a constant current of 1·5 knots, bearing 307°.

To lay the right course, we shift the departure point on the chart for the distance and direction the tide will take the boat off course during an hour's sailing:

■ We plot the direct course from NW Minquiers to Grand-Léjon.

■ From the NW Minquiers buoy, we plot a line representing an hour's current: that gives us point A, 1·5 nautical miles at 307° true from the buoy.

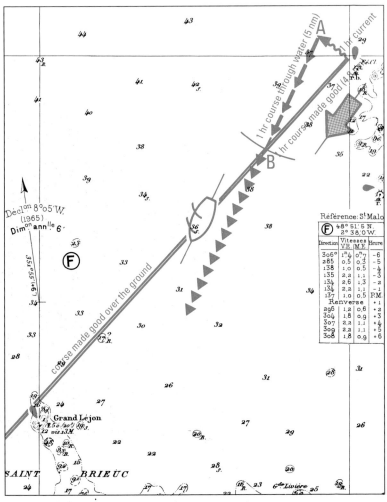

Heading of the boat in relation to the true course in a constant current.
(Chart of the SHOM.)

■ Taking point A as a centre, we mark an arc of radius 5 nautical miles (speed of the boat through the water). This arc cuts the direct course at point B.

■ We draw the line AB and measure the angle it makes with the north: 206°. This is the true heading.

Now it remains to calculate the compass course. Since the wind is NE, the boat will be running, and there will be no leeway. Thus we have:

True course	206°
Correction for variation	+ 7°
Compass course	= 213°

The tide is slightly against us. The speed over the ground is therefore not as great as the speed through the water. It is represented by the length of the vector NW Minquiers – point B, ie 4·8 knots instead of 5. It will therefore take a little longer to reach le Grand-Léjon than if there were no tide.

Fourth passage: with a variable tidal stream

We are at springs, and leaving the NW Minquiers buoy at HW – 6.

This time it is all too obvious that the chart inset shows that there will be considerable tidal variations in the hours to come. We shall have to calculate the bearing in relation to the whole of the journey: this means shifting the departure point to compensate for all the tidal changes that will take place along the way.

First of all we must estimate the time taken for the voyage. The wind is E, therefore abaft the beam, but weak. The boat will probably travel at about 4 knots. Is it possible to make the trip in about 4 hours?

To find out, we shift the departure point, taking into account the tidal variations in the next four hours:

1st	hour	:	1·4 knots at 306°
2nd	hour	:	0·5 knots at 285°
3rd	hour	:	1·0 knots at 138°
4th	hour	:	2·2 knots at 135°

From the theoretical point 4, we measure the distance to Grand-Léjon: 18·8 nautical miles – the actual distance to be covered through the water. Four hours is a bit short so add another hour of tide: 2·6 knots at 134°. From point 5, the distance is 19·3 nautical miles. Five hours is then more than we need, so we place our theoretical departure point between points 4 and 5. From there, we plot the line to le Grand-Léjon and measure the true course: 233°.

Since there is no leeway due to the wind, the compass course is:

$$233° + 7° = 240°$$

The boat will then follow the course over the ground shown on the chart. This is some way off the direct course, but tides being what they are, it is unquestionably the shortest route that could be found: in fact, the boat sailing in a constant heading will make the trip in a straight line on the water. It will have travelled 20·5 nautical miles over the ground, but only 19·3 nautical miles through the water.

Here, where there are dangers en route, it is a good idea to trace the route over the ground on the chart, so as to know where one is passing, and to be able to check progress.

Note that even when the wind makes it seem likely that tacking may be necessary, the calculations we have just gone through must

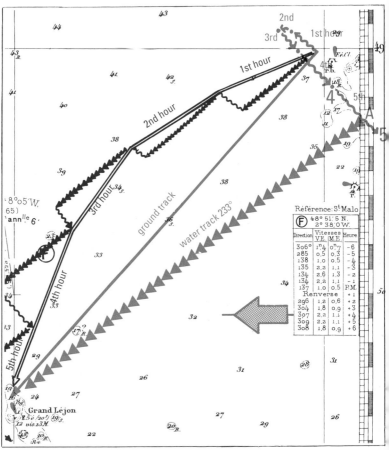

Heading of the boat in relation to a variable current
In principle, by calculating the course from point A, it ought to be able to pass le Grand-Léjon without difficulty. However, if the wind drops and the boat slows, then the trip will take longer than estimated. It might well be a good idea to allow for a quarter of an hour extra tide, and thus calculate the course from point 5.

on no account be omitted. Indeed, it might very well turn out that the compulsory detour imposed by the tide will allow you to make the trip on a close fetch, without having to tack at all.

However, all these problems are comparatively simple. We have supposed the speed of the boat to be constant. In reality, it varies continuously, in relation to the weather conditions for instance. This makes life much more complicated. The theory must constantly be adapted to suit the circumstances, and this will be the subject of the chapter dealing with the choice of route.

4

NAVIGATION
OFFSHORE

Dick Sand, apprentice on board the brigantine *Pilgrim*, making passage from Auckland to Valparaiso, is promoted captain as a result of dramatic events that resulted in the officers and almost all the crew perishing. Although near to despair, the boy is determined to bring his ship safe into harbour. Not knowing how to make an astronomical fix, Dick has to rely on dead reckoning alone, that is to say, an estimate of the course travelled each day based on the compass and log readings. Unfortunately, there is a treacherous villain on board who has managed to put a piece of iron under the ship's compass. This gives it a deviation of 45° East. The blackguard also arranges for the log line to break. Thereupon, a terrific storm ensues, driving the boat towards the SE, and then to the NE at a speed impossible to estimate. The upshot is that Dick Sand, having passed Cape Horn without realising it, and mistaking Tristan da Cunha for Easter Island, finally runs aground on the shores of Angola, believing he had arrived in Bolivia.

Such a colossal mistake in dead reckoning is without precedent in the annals of the sea, but that is the tale told by Jules Verne in *A Fifteen-Year-Old Captain*, one of the most gloriously botched-up novels of all time. Nonetheless, the work stands as a parable of navigation: no captain can expect to finish on target if the reckoning is out from the word go.

Nevertheless, provided that there are no blackguards on your boat, dead reckoning is the most accurate way of locating your position when out of sight of land, and it is the method we shall examine in detail in this chapter.

After studying dead reckoning, we shall consider the different techniques for finding your position accurately when approaching land. **The only real difficulty about navigation offshore is when it comes to making a landfall.** You don't have to have made a particularly long passage for this apparently simple procedure to become problematic: all that has to happen is for the fog to come up when you are a few cables out from land, or for you to be caught at night along a badly lit coast. These methods must be mastered therefore even if you have no intention of sailing offshore: while sailing out of sight of land is undoubtedly the dream of all sailors, it can quickly become a nightmare if you are not prepared and remains a risk every time a sailor sets out.

There can be no neglecting the other dream of the apprentice sailor: sailing by the stars. Navigating by the stars is only really of any use on long journeys, but knowing the basic principles is a pleasure in itself, and contributes to one's knowledge of the sea.

Dead reckoning

There are now two ways of navigating offshore. There are electronic position-fixing devices, which cost between two and twenty thousand pounds, and which allow you, as long as you have enough electrical power, to find out your position to within anything between about two nautical miles and 10m simply by pressing a button. There is also the old method of dead reckoning, which is as old as the sea itself. One thing is certain: **while electronic position-fixing is not absolutely necessary, dead reckoning is indispensable**.

Whatever the quality of equipment, there is always the possibility of a power failure, or, if the boat is struck by lightning for example, of electrical and electronic equipment being disabled or destroyed.

Dead reckoning is a method of calculating the course made good by the boat from its last known position. This is based on the distance run, on the estimated leeway and tidal stream and on the course followed.

Transferring the dead reckoning onto the chart – a process known as plotting the course made good – is a simple enough operation in itself. It consists of:

■ correcting the compass course by the amount of the variation, deviation and leeway, so as to obtain the true course;

■ from the true course, plotting the distance made good through the water, and marking on it the distance run;

■ finally, adjusting, if necessary, the position arrived at by the amount the boat has drifted because of the tidal stream.

This will then give you the course made good over the ground. In order to lay a course, the navigator had to think ahead and reckon on the conditions they might possibly encounter. When plotting the course made good, the navigator has to take into account what has actually happened, and what the conditions were like. Obviously, these are never quite as foreseen. Correctly assessing the information at hand in order to provide a dead reckoning is clearly the main difficulty, and requires a highly-developed feel for sea conditions.

This is the true test of the navigator's mettle. They must be both reserved but always on the alert. The chart table is their principal preserve, but then again, nothing that goes on on board escapes them. They observe everything, and make a note of even the most insignificant details. As much psychologist as technician, they know the character of all the helmsmen they have to deal with, and also what to expect of the boat at any given speed and under any sail.

Sea conditions, changes in the wind and weather are all of interest.

It is as if the navigator were conducting an ongoing inquiry and considering every incident from their own particular point of view. Even when a sudden lurch sends the crockery flying across the table, they are gathering useful information, and – undoubtedly – such is their curiosity that every time they poke their head out of the cabin, they check the quarter wave. Back in their bunk, they listen and ponder. Finally, the moment arrives, when, summing up all their observations and calculations, they put the point of the pencil on the chart and say 'We are here'.

How have they arrived at this decision? It is obviously not just a question of checking off the thousand and one details that allow them to arrive at a dead-reckoning position. Science is learned from books, but then it is not really an art either. At most, all we can do here is to lay out some basic principles to guide the beginning navigator. Of course, the portrait of the navigator as an artist lost in prophetic contemplation should not be taken too seriously: a dead-reckoning is as much the product of the entire crew, especially when they are used to sailing together and all have some experience in navigation.

Appraising the available information

Having an accurate last known position available is the most important factor in dead reckoning or when estimating position. If you make a mistake with the first button, you'll get caught with your pants down, to mix a metaphor.

Even when nobody had any intention of sailing out of sight of land, the navigator must always be on the alert. It is not strictly necessary to be making a fix feverishly every twenty minutes, when visibility is perfect and the forecast is for cool, changeable weather; however, if there is any danger of fog, then it is a good idea to take a fix every hour at least, and at every change of heading.

Is the boat being kept on course?

Is the helm following the course accurately? A good question. Keep a discreet eye on the course from the cabin using the hand-held compass. Some helms don't like having the wind dead astern, and always tend to come on to a broad reach; others, close-hauled, get too close to the wind, which gives a lot more leeway than you might have expected: note differences of this sort. One helm, possibly a novice, always steers 5° too much to starboard, so give them a course 5° to port – and so on. If the boat is yawing too much, then the sails will have to be trimmed to make things easier for the helm.

When close to the wind, do not give a course – this will make dead reckoning easier. If one is following a course in these conditions, and the wind varies, then it becomes impossible to estimate drift with any degree of accuracy. Steering as the wind dictates means that the leeway remains constant, which is what counts.

What really matters on this point of sailing is that the helm should be able to say honestly what average heading you have followed. Inexperience is not so enduring a problem as pig-headedness.

Leeway

The strength of the wind, point of sailing, sea conditions, the tuning of the boat, and the skill of the helm are all variables that have to be taken into account when estimating leeway. Always check leeway at every opportunity, but don't tell the helm what you are doing, as they will concentrate on keeping the course during the check, thus rendering the exercise useless. The thing to check is what the helm *is* doing rather than what they *can* do when under constant surveillance.

Distance run

Logs are fairly reliable provided that their strengths and weaknesses are taken into account: some are optimistic, and some tend more towards caution. Most of them are inaccurate at lower speeds.

The vane of a patent log has to be carefully watched. It might have suffered a knock since last used, and could then turn faster (or more slowly) than it should. It can also catch up in seaweed and jam as a result. Keep an eye on the dial and take readings regularly – every hour, for instance. Get into the habit of making a mental estimate of the speed of the boat, so that you will be able to assess the distance run if the log breaks down.

Electronic logs are almost always equipped with an alarm which sounds whenever the propeller or the paddle wheel stop turning. Doppler logs are practically unaffected by seaweed and other floating debris.

The tidal stream

The actual route over the ground does not always correspond to what you thought it was.

ground track

Tidal stream predictions are all very well, but personal observation is better. The information given on tides is only accurate up to a certain point, and, as is well known, the wind can upset all the calculations anyway. Passing a lobster pot or a buoy is a useful chance to check the direction and approximate strength of the tidal stream. When an exact position is required, such as in fog near land, it is well worth a detour to take a closer look at any fixed object.

Offshore, it can be difficult to determine the direction in which the boat is moving. The leadline, or a fishing line with a heavy weight, can then come in handy. Drop the line, giving it plenty of slack; when it goes taut the angle the line makes with the stern is fair indication of the direction of movement in relation to the bottom.

Apart from the tidal streams covered in the chapter on navigation inshore, it is a good idea to know the general streams whose strength is given in nautical miles covered per 24 hours in the Pilot and other nautical publications. One should also take note of the surface currents created when the winds are strong and blow in the same direction for long periods. Tables can be found in the Pilot books.

The log book

The entries on the ship's log can be followed in reverse back over the course run, rather in the way that Theseus found his way out of the labyrinth. All the details used in laying the course must be entered: courses (the one asked for and the one actually followed), the log readings, strength and direction of the wind, sea conditions, name of the helm. All changes should also be noted: going about, changes of sail, changes in the weather, fixes taken (and how they were made), along with any ships met. Nothing must be judged insignificant on an a priori basis.

It is wiser to list only the bare data: that is to say, compass course, rather than true course, the figure read from the log rather than the distance run, and so on. If each individual adds his or her own personal interpretation in the log book, then the risk of error is multiplied by the number of people on board, and the facts can thereby be irrevocably distorted.

The ship's log must also be kept scrupulously up to date, even when dead reckonings are not expected to be made. It is always possible that a reckoning might have to be made. Furthermore, if there is an accident, then the ship's log can be invaluable as evidence of what actually happened. In France, it is compulsory to keep a log for all boats of category 3 and up (ie sailing over 20 miles from shore); it is certainly a good idea for categories 4 and 5 (over 5 miles from shore).

If the boat is equipped with a Loran, Decca, Satnav, GPS or other position finder, the log must still be kept up to date, and the position given must be noted at least four times a day. This position can then serve as the starting point for dead reckoning in case of instrument malfunction or failure.

The uncertainty principle

No matter how great the navigator's flair and precision may be, dead reckoning can seldom give an accurate position. There is a degree of uncertainty in all data, and thus the position is the sum of all those uncertainties.

This total can vary according to the conditions encountered. Sailing in an area with little or no tide (or where the tidal streams are precisely known), and running free with a steady, moderate wind on a calm sea, the margin of error is probably as low as 4% of the distance run. On the other hand, if you are tacking in light weather and

105

unfavourable currents, or have had to heave to in bad weather, then the margin of error can easily be 10% and higher. If you prefer, you may apply these percentage errors to the estimated time required for the passage, rather than to your estimated speed.

When a passage has been made in a straight line, then the area of uncertainty can be marked on the chart with some degree of precision: it is a quadrilateral, longer than it is broad if there is more reason to doubt the distance run than the course followed or broader than it is long if it is the course rather than the distance that seems open to question. If you have had to tack, however, then the area can only best be represented as a circle, whose diameter corresponds to the maximum amount of possible error. It is assumed for the purposes of calculation that one is in the middle of this circle, but of course, you could be anywhere within it.

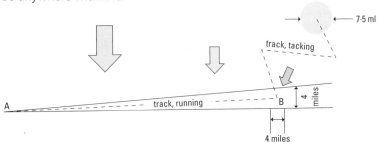

From A to B, the boat has followed a course with the wind free. In order to calculate the quadrilateral of uncertainty, uncertainty over course (eg 4 nautical miles) must be distinguished from uncertainty over distance (eg 3 nautical miles). From B onwards, because the wind has changed direction, it becomes difficult to maintain the distinction. To make things simpler, the area of uncertainty is taken to be a circle, whose diameter is equal to the maximum degree of uncertainty (here, for example, 7·5 nautical miles).

As the distance covered increases, the circle of uncertainty grows, and the reckoning becomes more and more open to error. Obviously, it must be updated at every possible opportunity, particularly when landfall is made. Running fixes and running a line of soundings are rather old-fashioned methods, but are not bad for gathering information, and a radio direction-finder can also help. Meeting another boat can also be useful. All these methods allow for greater precision, but the value of this information is minimal unless the actual reckoning is relatively accurate. This is the most important technique to master.

Transferred position line

The position in question is a geometrical one: either a bearing or a position circle, or a measure of height by an astronomical fix.

The principle of the transfer is very simple. We know that at least two of the points must be recognised if a fix is to be made: the point where our bearings cross gives our position. But if there is only one bearing available, it can always be kept in reserve until another is found. The first position line is then transferred according to the course run: it then intersects with the second. However, the fix obtained by this method is only accurate if the dead reckoning has been correctly kept up.

A fix can be thereby be made with transferred position lines from two marks. At 8 o'clock a lighthouse A is seen at 120°. At midday, lighthouse A is out of sight, but we can now see lighthouse B on a bearing of 60°. By dead reckoning, we have run 18 miles at 40°. At 0800, the boat was somewhere along the line Ac. To transfer this line, the simplest thing to do is to transfer landmark A 18 nautical miles along a bearing of 40°. From there, draw a line parallel to Ac. The transferred position line cuts the line Bd at point F and that is the position of the boat at noon. It is possible starting from F to run through the procedure backwards and find out what the position of the boat was at 0800: point E. This also constitutes a useful double check to see that the transfer was correctly done.

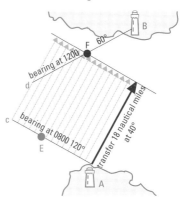

Fix by transferred position line on two marks.
While transferring the bearing Ac, the area of uncertainty introduced into the dead reckoning between 0800 and midday must be taken into account.

The method can also be applied with even less data. It is possible to make a fix by successive bearings on the same mark – making a running fix. At midnight, we have the lighthouse P at 15°. Three hours later, we can still only see lighthouse P, and this time at a bearing of 64°. By dead reckoning, we have covered 12 miles at 290° during these three hours. The bearing Pa, shifted by the twelve miles of the reckoning, cuts the bearing Pb at point M, and this gives the boat's position at 0300.

This system of transferring position lines on the chart has great potential. There is nothing to pre-

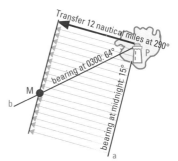

Running fix by different bearings on the same landmark.
Here, equally, the transfer of bearing Pa is also subject to uncertainty affecting the dead reckoning between midnight and 0300. Three bearings in succession reduce this area of uncertainty by creating a cocked hat.

vent us from transferring the same position line several times in succession, making it tack with the boat and using it in several different positions.

A detailed example will show the kind of working necessary to make a landfall using this kind of method.

On the road to Groix

It is dawn on a June morning. Fog has come down during the night and is still persisting in large patches, although the sun is breaking through in places. We are coming in from Belle-Île, and want to enter the port of Lorient. The wind is NNE. Because of bad visibility, it is better to go round the west end of Groix and be able to make landfall on an open, easily-recognisable coast: the point of Pen-a-Men.

We are making a course of 330° true. At 0500 we catch sight of Groix through the haze, but cannot identify anything precisely. It is time to plot our dead reckoning on the chart. We estimate the margin of error to be 6% or 7%, which gives us, taking the distance run since Belle-Île into account, a circle of about 2 nautical miles in diameter. This circle is drawn, and in its centre (the estimated position of the boat), the time of the fix (0500) and the log reading (53·2) are entered.

At 0512, we see the Pen-a-Men lighthouse for a moment in a clear patch. Its bearing is taken immediately: 50° true. This is bearing I. When this position line is plotted on the chart, it shows that the estimated position (EP) was somewhat optimistic: we have not covered as much ground as we thought. The area of uncertainty is no longer the circle, but only a sector of it, length equal to the diameter of the circle, and width equal to the possible uncertainty of the bearing. The boat should be at point A.

It is nonetheless wise to reckon on being in the most unfavourable position, that is at point B. To clear Pen-a-Men from point B, we reckon we still have 1·3 nautical miles to go, on a bearing of 330°, before we go about. We shall therefore go about when the log reaches 55. This margin is good enough to avoid any risk of hitting the point, but will let us pass close enough to have a chance of seeing it.

At 0525 we go about, and proceed on a heading of 70° on port tack.

The minutes pass. We ought to be close to the point by now, and everyone is screwing up their eyes. Gradually, in the morning mist, the dark mass of the coastline looms up. We spot the lighthouse, taking its bearing at 145° true. This is bearing II. The time is now 0548, log 56·7.

Since we went about we have therefore run 1·7 nautical miles at 70°. We must now transfer bearing I by the distance run, so we move the lighthouse itself by 1·3 nautical miles at 330° and then 1·7 nautical miles at 70°, and from the new point (PI), we draw a line parallel to bearing I. This line cuts the bearing II at C, which gives us the position of the boat.

As we can still see the coast quite clearly, it is a good idea to take a third bearing to get a proper fix. We wait for a little while: the bigger the angle between the last two bearings, the more accurate the fix will be. The lighthouse is soon out of sight, but the point itself remains visible. We take its bearing at 205° just before it disappears. It is 0555, log 57·3. We have covered 0·6 nautical miles from point C.

We plot the new bearing, which is bearing III. We then transfer by 0·6 nautical miles the two bearings that have given us fix C (P2 and P3). We obtain a cocked hat, and the boat probably lies inside it.

For the sake of curiosity, we can amuse ourselves by retracing the course we have covered from the middle of the hat. This shows that when we saw Pen-a-Men for the first time, we were in fact at point E.

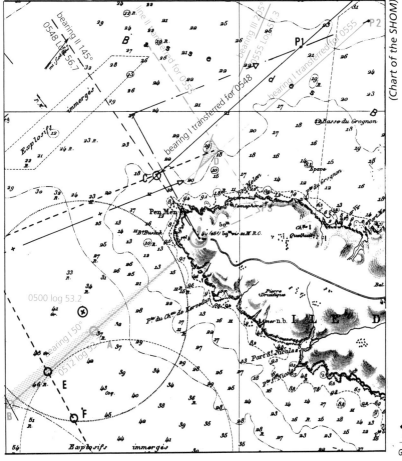

(Chart of the SHOM)

We also discover that at 0500, when we traced our circle, supposing ourselves to be somewhere near the centre of it, we were in fact at point F, on the outer limit of the error we allowed for.

Navigating in fog

When everything disappears into the mist, the sort of uncertainty we are dealing with changes. Even if the dead reckoning has been kept accurately, and we know exactly where we are, the fact that we can

1 *The foredeck hand swings the lead with a pendulum motion...*

2 *...throws it as far forward as possible...*

3 *...and lets the line run out through finger and thumb.*

4 *The lead must be on the bottom when the boat passes over it.*

no longer see anything requires that a certain number of precautions be taken: speed must be reduced, the foghorn must be sounded regularly, and we must keep an ear out. The main risk is that of colliding with another boat. Moreover, if about to make a landfall, we must hold off and wait until we can see a little more clearly.

However, even in the fog, there is one point of reference that remains reliable: the sea bottom. The bottom is a well defined stretch of ground, covered with plains and valleys, various sorts of plants and deeper channels. It provides information of all kinds, and has the useful characteristic of rising when land is near: a handy warning.

It is therefore possible to make landfall without being able to see your hand in front of your face, as long as you are in an area with easily identifiable features on the sea bottom, and you take accurate soundings.

The procedure to follow varies according to the nature of the bottom: sometimes there is a line of soundings that will keep you clear of all the dangers along the coast. Sometimes you need to fix position by running a line of soundings. However, everything depends on the depth sounding equipment you have available.

The echo sounder and the leadline

The echo sounder and the leadline are clearly very different instruments. The echo sounder can take soundings at great depth and gives accurate and continuous readings. The leadline is really only accurate in shallow water (less than 15m) and only gives information at intervals. For depths greater than 20m, the most that one can know is whether the boat is between different depth markings.

It is therefore impossible to use a lead and an echo sounder in the same way. The one allows you to figure out your position with great accuracy, the other registers the approach of dangers, allowing avoiding action to be taken. Another important difference is that the use of the echo sounder needs no special expertise on the part of the operator, while the use of the lead calls for some experience and practice.

When an exact depth has to be taken in shallow water, the procedure is as follows. The line should be ready in a bucket, or flaked on the deck. To throw the lead you should usually stand on the leeward side of the boat, about amidships. Hold the lead in the leeward hand, with the weight just above the water, then set it swinging with a pendulum motion and throw it as far forward as possible, so that it hits the bottom before the boat overtakes it. The faster the boat is going, the further the lead must be thrown. Some champions can throw it 15m. Take care not to hit anyone with the lead when swinging it.

As soon as the lead hits the water, it makes a splash that leaves a ripple. When you come up to this ripple, the line is held straight up and down to mark the depth. If the lead brings up sand, the bottom is sandy; if it brings up mud, the bottom is mud; if it brings up gold, stop and drop anchor at once.

As soon as the water gets fairly deep, then the result becomes rather hit and miss, since the boat has generally passed before the lead line reaches the bottom. If it is vital to get an exact sounding, then the boat must either slow or stop.

On a beat, stopping half way through a tack with the jib backed is quite handy for slowing the boat down to get a sounding. Up to 20m, the lead is particularly useful for finding the depth contours. The technique is then somewhat different. If you want to know, for instance, when you will cross the 20m line, you first make ready the required length of line (20m plus the depth of water above chart datum for that hour of the tide, plus the freeboard and the height of the stern rail to which the line is fastened). One of the crew then throws the lead from the bows of the boat as far forward as possible. The line must be vertical when you pass on a level with the ripple (if it isn't, you're going too fast). Once you have passed the ripple, haul in the line, and you will be able to tell by the tallow smeared on the bottom whether you have touched bottom or not.

Sounding in deep water

In order to be of real use in deep water cruising, an echo sounder must be capable of registering depths to at least 100m. If it can do that, then it can supply all kinds of precious information far offshore. When crossing the channel between Torquay and Paimpol, for example, a dead reckoning which has become pretty shaky owing to periods of calm and a certain amount of beating can be brought up to date again when crossing Hurd Deep, when the sounder will suddenly indicate depths of over 100m for a short distance.

Coming in to make landfall at Penmarc'h in thick weather, in an area littered with rather nasty rocks, you know you have nothing to fear as long as the 100m line has not been reached. Making a landfall at Groix – described in the previous section by way of illustrating the method of transferring position lines – could have been done in quite a different way, if the sounder had been used. The moment you sight the lighthouse at Pen-a-Men for the first time, the echo-sounder will give you an exact fix immediately. Thanks to the bearing, we know that the boat is somewhere along the line drawn from the lighthouse, but as the sounder gives a depth of 45m, we must be somewhere close to point E.

These examples give a simple idea of what can be done with the echo sounder. Certainly, such a piece of equipment is at least as useful as the DF aerial. Sounders are, furthermore, almost all equipped with an alarm which can be set to a specific depth. This is very useful for tacking safely along the coast, when there is a depth contour running more or less parallel to the coast.

Following a depth contour

Following a depth contour with an echo sounder is child's play. However, as we have seen, it is equally possible to follow one with a lead line. Obviously, the boat must not be going too fast, nor must it be tacking. In practice, following a depth contour is generally a matter of not moving too far away from it.

In thick weather, it is possible to reach the Cochon tower by following the 10m depth contour. (Chart of the SHOM)

113

Let us take the example of the approach to Groix for the last time, and examine the profile of the depth contours around Pen-a-Men point. Even if the fog had got thicker, it would have been perfectly possible to go round the point in perfect safety by following the 20m contour, which would give us a wide berth around all the possible dangers.

Another example is the entry into the port of Concarneau. Suppose we were caught by the fog 1·5 nautical miles to the south of the Cochon beacon. We take soundings and find less than 10m of water, so we immediately set course NW to find the 10m line again, which we then follow, always leaving it slightly to starboard. It is thereby easy to arrive at the Cochon beacon, and from there enter the channel by dead reckoning, keeping the 5m contours to either side. The example which follows on the next page was taken from the log of a cruise to Cornwall.

Running a line of soundings

There is not always a depth contour that will lead us directly to where we are going. On many occasions we have to proceed step by step, trying first of all to reach a spot that can be identified with some degree of certainty. This allows us then to fix our position before going any further.

To make a fix by using soundings, the dead reckoning usually has to be made by running a line of soundings. To do this, take a piece of squared tracing paper, which can then be moved over the chart parallel to the meridians or the parallels. This effectively forms a blank chart with north at the top.

As we approach landfall, the track made good over the ground is plotted on the tracing paper, along with the soundings taken. Always pay attention to the scale of the chart when marking the track and the soundings. The next step is then to move the tracing paper over the chart, and to try to make the soundings you have marked match up with the ones on the chart. You may find your position very quickly and very accurately, but things may not be so easy and you will then have to backtrack and begin again, always keeping the dead reckoning up to date…

Musings of a fog-bound navigator

To follow the pilot, turn to the chart on pages 116–17.

My name is Jézéquel. Remember me?
The famous Glénans sailing school was so impressed by my earlier writings that they offered to lend me their Bermudan-rigged cutter, *Sereine*, 12·5m long and 13 tonnes displacement.

I accepted instantly, especially since Sophie is part of the crew, along with eight others. The boat has no motor, and is rather short on modern navigation equipment, but it has a good electronic log and a depth sounder which is accurate up to 100m. The compass has been corrected recently. The boat is well found, and the crew has already spent a week at sea together so they are well settled in. I should be able to head for the Scilly Isles from Salcombe.

Having left our charming mooring about noon, we beat across Plymouth Sound and pass the Lizard some 24 hours later. The weather forecast is depressing. The Falmouth Coastguard come through on channel 67 threatening light winds and fog banks. Sophie is pestering me to get to the Mermaid pub on the Scilly Isles, so all in all, I think it will be worth persevering.

In fact I do not think we'll be able to make it across the traffic separation lanes between Land's End and the Scilly Isles for another 12 hours or so. There are no danger spots along the way to Wolf Rock, and I should be able to hear the foghorn at Wolf Rock if the fog persists. With a bit of luck the fog will have lifted anyway by the time we get that far.

So off we head, westwards, closehauled and at a rather leisurely pace. At about 1800 the wind drops entirely and the fog thickens up further. I take a quick look at the *Tidal Streams Atlas*, and I reckon we're being taken out to sea. The average current over these last 6 hours will have been 1 knot, at about 135°. The freight ship foghorns sound ever gloomier, as they get closer. The depth sounder indicates 80 or 90m, which confirms my feeling that we're drifting westwards. I try for an RDF position, but I can't tune the receiver quite precisely enough: I suspect the receiver must have taken a whack last week in the heavy swell. Finally, the RDF gear packs in completely.

I call up Falmouth Coastguard on channel 16 to get a weather forecast. A nasal voice informs me that the fog covers the whole area from the Lizard to the Scilly Isles and they don't know when it'll lift. With luck, the temperature will drop at night and improve the visibility.

Night falls at 2100, and a light westerly breeze arrives. The boat finally starts to make headway, but we still can't see any more than 50m. At 2200, no change. Sophie seems more interested in her bearded co-crew than in the skipper, which is pretty frustrating. Time for an executive decision…

Let us summarise.

We are in 80-90m of water, making 3·5 knots in the fog; I have an idea that merchant shipping is in the area. My dead reckoning has been running for 10 hours, so I'm not really certain of our position. Certainly we are drifting out towards the Atlantic. The only thing I don't know is what time the fog will lift.

(Chart no 6848 of the SHOM.)

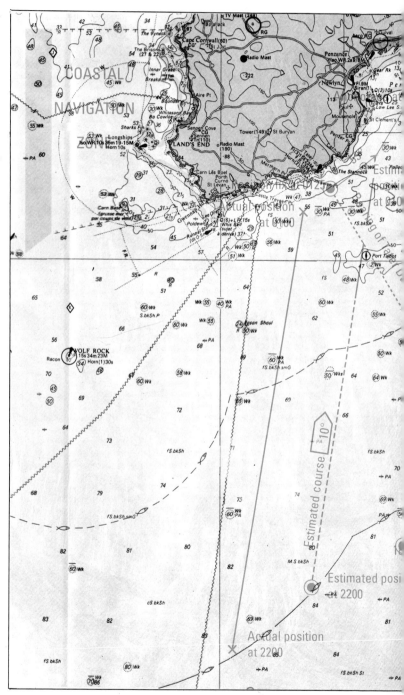

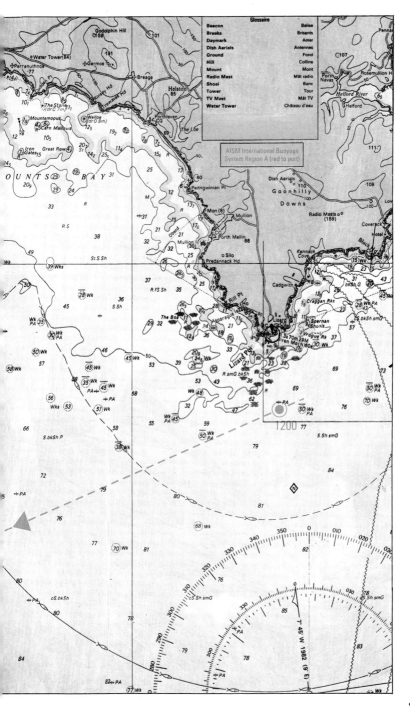

Glossaire

Beacon	Balise
Breaks	Brisants
Daymark	Amer
Dish Aerials	Antennes
Ground	Fond
Hill	Colline
Mount	Mont
Radio Mast	Mât radio
Shoal	Banc
Tower	Tour
TV Mast	Mât TV
Water Tower	Château d'eau

AISM International Buoyage
System Region A (red to port)

Putting it another way, the only thing I do know is that trying to hit a small group of scattered islands in this fog, across shipping lanes is out of the question.

My dead reckoning puts me towards the western edge of Penzance Bay. Inside the bay, which is 5 miles wide approximately the bottom slopes gently upward; so long as I stay in at least 20m of water, there is no danger. I decide to turn round until we reach a depth of 30m and to drop the light dinghy anchor, on 20m of chain and 100m of light line. Once we are safely anchored, I'll sound the fog warning bell until the fog clears. There's not even any point trying to get into Penzance harbour.

At 2200 I ask the helm to head round to 10° so we can find a depth of 50m and get a fix on the foghorn at Tater Du. Even if we are further west than we reckon, we should be quite safe so long as we stay in 50m or more. If we are further east, the situation is no worse, because the 50m depth contour has no hazards on it. The key job at this stage is to watch the depth sounder, so I ask Sophie to keep an eye on it and sing out the depths regularly.

At 0100 there is the sound of a fog signal to our starboard, two blasts every 30 seconds. The depth sounder shows 60m, but I'm sure I hear the sound of surf breaking to port. Check the chart and the *List of Lights*: this can only be Tater Du. At this point the 50m contour is only a mile from the coast.

I need to leave this headland to port if we are to get into Penzance Bay. The helm heads 55°, which is about the same as the 50m contour around Tater Du. I am now increasingly confident of our position: we must be to the east of Tater Du. If we follow the 50m contour precisely, adding 2m for the height of the tide, we'll clear Tater Du with no difficulty. I therefore ask for us to stick to a depth sounder reading of 52m.

A bearing on the foghorn would help confirm our position. I ask a couple of other crew members to check my reading on the hand bearing compass. Our estimates vary by about 25°, too much really to be of any help. I abandon this attempt and fall back on the trusty depth sounder.

Right! 52m on the display. And the wind is coming round to SSW, allowing us to free the sheets and follow our desired course nicely off the wind. This way, I can just use the 52m contour as my guide. Nothing else counts. 53…, 54…, 55…, the helm turns a little to the left; 51…, 50…, 49 and goes back to the right.

The Tater Du signal continues to sound to our left, then suddenly a hole in the fog gives us a glimpse of the light itself, at 330°. Eureka! Certainty! It is 0125, and I make an entry in the log. There is little tide, and the boat is heading downwind. I should be able to keep going, well clear of land, and then get closer in to 30m where we can drop anchor. *Sereine* keeps up a steady 5 knots even in this

118

light breeze, so I drop the foresail to reduce our speed to 3·5 knots. The depth sounder dead reckoning continues. The crew keeps its ears pricked. Conversation is in whispers. The boat glides through flat water, too fast for my taste, too slow for Sophie's.

As the water gets shallower, we travel ever more slowly, until at 0230, we drop anchor in 27m of water. The crew head off to their bunks, exhausted, except for two unlucky ones who have to stay up to ring the fog bell every so often. Sophie is one of those who draw the short straw. I drop off to sleep, pretty confident of having moored in the middle of Penzance Bay. At daybreak, Sophie shakes me from my slumber to show me a familiar shape emerging from the mist: good old St Michael's Mount.

Radio direction-finding

The log and soundings are not the only means for establishing position in bad conditions. There are also a certain number of radioelectrical navigational aids, which can be of use in keeping a check on the boat's position. The most commonly used in amateur sailing is radio direction-finding, whose basic principles are simple enough: with the help of the appropriate type of radio receiver, the bearings of various transmitters are established, and these bearings, when plotted on the chart, allow a fix to be made.

Radio beacons

The transmitters used in radio direction-finding are known as radio beacons, which transmit a specific signal on a predetermined frequency on the long-wave band.

In order to avoid overcrowding the frequencies, radio beacons usually transmit their identification signals three to six times in succession on the same frequency. They transmit in turn and always in the same order. The signal transmitted by each beacon lasts one minute in all and consists of:

■ the identification signal of the beacon, a group of two or three Morse letters, repeated several times for 22 seconds;

■ a long dash lasting 25 seconds;

■ the identification signal repeated once or twice for approximately 8 seconds;

■ a silent period of at least 5 seconds, after which the next beacon comes in.

The characteristics of the radio beacons are given in the Admiralty *List of Radio Signals*. There are also radio beacon maps which are convenient and adequate for small boats, and the signals are also given in *Reed's Nautical Almanac*, or, for the French Channel and Atlantic coasts, in the *Almanach du Marin Breton*.

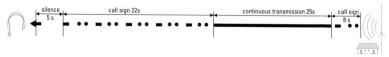

Form of the message for the radio beacon for the cape of Antifer (call sign TI).
The basic form applies to all other RDF transmitters.

The receiver

The receiver is a radio set with a directional aerial plugged into it, referred to as a DF aerial. The aerial used on board small boats is a piece of ferrite rod usually attached to a small hand-bearing compass.

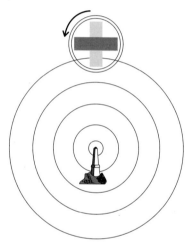

If the DF aerial is in the position marked in blue, then the sound is at its weakest; if it is in the position marked in black, the sound is at its strongest.

When the receiver is tuned to the frequency of a radio beacon, then the radio wave transmitted by the beacon induces a current in the DF aerial, with an intensity that varies according to the position of the aerial. This is exactly what happens in an ordinary transistor radio, which must be orientated in relation to the transmitting aerial if you want to hear the music properly. The strength is at its maximum – and consequently the sound itself at a maximum – when the ferrite rod is at right angles to the direction of the transmitter. It is this null point that you want to find in order to get the bearing of the beacon: it is a more precise indication of direction than trying to distinguish the point at which the signal is at maximum strength. When the 'null' – the arc of the weakest signal – has some breadth, you rotate the aerial slowly to find the edges of the 'null', and the bearing of the radio beacon lies in the middle of this arc.

Publications give the frequency of the radio beacons in kilohertz (kHz); the dial of the receiver is often graduated in metres, so that it indicates the wavelength. To convert from frequency to wavelength, apply the formula:

$$L \text{ (in metres)} = \frac{300,000}{F \text{ (in kHz)}}$$

The magnetic bearing is read directly from the compass. Note that some aerials are not fitted with a compass, but rather only a rotating loop which gives the heading of the radio beacon in relation to the axis of the boat. In order to obtain the true bearing of the radio beacon, all that then needs to be done is to add this relative bearing to the true heading of the boat (subtracting 360° if necessary).

The bearing obtained is accurate 180° either way, that is to say you do not know at which end of the aerial the beacon lies. Some receivers are equipped with a device which can tell you the direction of the beacon, but, with the exception of a few unusual situations (radio beacon on a light vessel in dense fog), it should be fairly obvious what the bearing is.

When the boat is a very long way away from the radio beacon, another step can be taken: the navigator must apply half-convergency correction. This enables the bearing to be plotted (the bearing being an arc of a great circle) as a straight line on a Mercator chart. In practice, on board a small boat far from the coast, radio bearings soon become inaccurate and, generally speaking, they become unusable by the time you would want to apply half-convergency correction to them anyway.

It is enough to say that 50 nautical miles away from a radio beacon, the maximum correction would be of the order of 1·4 nautical miles; at 100 nautical miles, 3·7 miles; at 200 nautical miles, 5·3 miles. The correction is nil for north and south bearings, because, as you will remember, the arcs of a great circle, which make up the meridian, appear as straight lines in Mercator's projection.

The value of radio bearings

For various reasons, DF radio bearings are rarely accurate. Some of these reasons pertain to the way in which the radio waves travel; others are connected with the process of reception itself.

Wave propagation

Radio waves do not always travel in a straight line: they can be deflected by an uneven surface and can be refracted when they pass obliquely from the land to the sea. The direct wave can be subject to interference from an indirect wave reflected by the ionosphere (night error).

Error due to refraction can be as much as 5° when the bearing cuts the

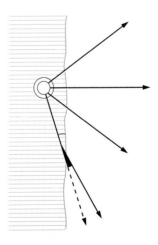

When radio waves reach the coast at a shallow angle, there can be considerable refraction.

coast at an angle of less than 30°. Night error is often greater still: it is worst at sunrise and at sunset, so these are bad times to take radio bearings. The best time is in the middle of the day.

Reception

A variety of factors combine to create difficulties at the receiving end. In the first place, radio waves can be deflected around the aerial by any magnetic objects on board. This is particularly so in steel or concrete boats: it is then necessary to use a fixed aerial, whose margin for error has been calculated in advance by making a deviation curve as for fixed compasses. On other boats, a directional aerial can be used, but it must always be kept away from anything magnetic. Beware of loudspeakers or earphones (especially if they are of the stethoscope variety). If you tend to hold the aerial close to you, then the headphones should be worn behind the head, and not down on the chest.

The quality of the receiver can also create problems and especially its selectivity. If several transmitters are interfering with each other, reception becomes very poor (not to say rather harsh on the ears) if the set has poor selectivity.

Rough seas can also be a source of major error. It is impossible to hear anything in the trough of a wave, and there is consequently a risk of mistaking an incidental null point for a real one. In short, the skill of the operator is a determining factor in deciding the accuracy of the bearing. If the bearing is to be correct, constant practice is required as well as enormous powers of concentration – not to mention a strong stomach.

Eventually, it has to be accepted that even in the best conditions, it is difficult to give a sound estimate of the accuracy of a bearing. If the time of day is right, the reception clear and null zone only around 5°, one can reckon on a discrepancy of 2° either way in fine weather, and 5° in a rough sea. If the reception is muzzy and the null zone wide (10° to 20°), one cannot really hope for an accuracy any greater than +/- 4° in fine weather and +/- 7° or 8° in a rough sea. In really bad conditions, the potential degree of error is generally impossible to assess.

How to make a radio fix

To make a more or less accurate fix, it is a good idea to take several bearings on each radio beacon, and then the most likely one is chosen for each (note: this is not necessarily the average). In good conditions, three bearings on each beacon are probably sufficient, but it may be necessary to get five or six to get an accurate fix. The bearings should not all be taken in quick succession, but rather at an interval of a couple of hours, transferring the fix by the distance run in the meantime.

Since each beacon only transmits every six minutes, you have to reckon on taking 30 to 45 minutes to make a fix. This is why good concentration and the ability to cope with seasickness are important factors in the accuracy of the fix. Concentration is easier if you have earphones, which cut you off from what is going on around you to some extent, but the whole job can be much quicker and simpler if you have a set with two

radio-fixing without method can make you old before your time...

different receiving circuits – you can then pass from one band to another at the touch of a button. On a one-circuit receiver, searching for frequencies is frustrating and time-consuming. (A useful tip is to mark the frequencies on the dial with a Chinagraph pencil.) For the following example, it just so happens that we are using a double-circuit receiver.

A boat coming from the Fastnet rock is making for Swansea. The sea is heavy and the visibility is poor. As the coast comes up, the navigator decides to get a radio fix to make the dead reckoning position on the chart more accurate. This fix has a potential error reckoned at 7% of the course covered – or a circle of discrepancy 12·5 nautical miles in diameter.

The radio beacons available are: Tuskar Rock (to the SE of Ireland), Mizen Head (SW of Ireland), South Bishop (to the west of Wales), Round Island (on the Isles of Scilly), Lundy Island (in the Bristol Channel) and Creac'h (on Ushant).

They are distributed in the following manner:

| | Frequency: | |
Minutes	308 kHz	296·5kHz
0		Tuskar Rock
1	Mizen Head	
2		South Bishop
3	Round Island	
4		Lundy Island
5	Creac'h	

By tuning the set to these two frequencies, it is possible to pick up the beacons in this order: Mizen Head, South Bishop, Round Island, Lundy Island.

You can then take two minutes' rest, as there is no point using Tuskar Rock, because it is too far away, as is Creac'h, over the other side of Cornwall (the radio waves can be distorted as they pass over land).

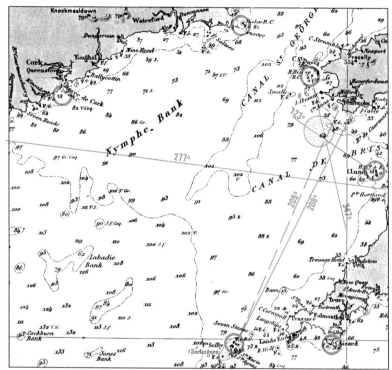

Radio fix for entry into the Bristol Channel. According to the dead reckoning, the boat is in the dotted circle. The radio bearings enable a more exact position to be fixed, but these bearings are only to be regarded as an aid to DR.

In 24 minutes, we get the following bearings:
Mizen Head at: 270°, 275°/277°, 286°/283°/273°
South Bishop at: 346°/349°/356°/345°, 348°
Round Island at: 198°,197°/210°/208°, 210°/207°, 206°
Lundy Island at: 120°/127°/128°/117°

Some of the beacons have been picked up twice in the same transmission, except for Lundy Island, which is not coming through clearly.

Now that the bearings have been taken, a little thought is needed to choose the most likely ones.

Mizen Head: the bearings vary a lot – we choose the average (277°), but without much confidence, since there is a difference of 16° between the highest and lowest readings.

South Bishop: we will keep 347°, as the 356° bearing seems an accident. The average would be 349°.

Round Island: 208° is chosen, since it is the average of the five figures, and the 197° and 198° readings are probably wrong.

Lundy Island: same proceedings as for Mizen Head – we take the average reading (123°).

These bearings are now plotted on the chart, and the result analysed:

The bearing of Mizen Head – 277° – is certainly wrong. For the reading to be right, there would have to be an error of at least 40° for Lundy Island, which is quite near. Besides, it also disagrees with the DR. It looks as if we must be to the west of the bearing of Round Island, which would indicate that the bearings of 197° and 198° were not all that far out. We therefore average out the bearings of Round Island: that gives us 205°.

At first glance, the cocked hat formed with the bearings of Lundy and South Bishop is almost too good to be true. However, taking the bearing of Round Island into account, we may reasonably assume that the boat is a little to the east of the cocked hat, so we may see the Helwick light vessel a little sooner than the dead reckoning would lead us to believe.

Homing on a radio beacon

When there is a radio beacon close to the port you are heading for, or on the course you are following, then it is quite simple to use this beacon as your heading. All you have to do is to keep an eye on the course. Some radio beacons are designed for precisely this sort of thing – they give out a different signal depending on whether you are to one side of the line of the channel or in line with it.

You must be certain that you can home in without running into any dangers along the way – that is to say, if there are no rocks between you and the beacon. It is, for instance, quite possible to home in on the beacon at Round Island if you are coming in from the north, but you should never do so if coming from the south: look at the chart and you'll see why.

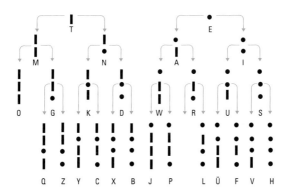

Morse code made easy
For a dot, look right; for a dash, look left. It might be useful to copy this table out on a larger sheet of paper and stick it up in the chart room.

Conclusion

As we have seen, even in perfect conditions, RDF will give you a margin of error of some 5°. You cannot rely on your bearings being exact.

Radio fixes are, all in all, a useful aid, but it would be very dangerous to rely on them and nothing else. The Pilot puts it very nicely:

> **The navigator should not trust blindly indications of position given by one navigational aid alone (radioelectric or otherwise).** *It is the navigator's duty, taking account of the degree of precision he can expect from any of these aids when used in combination with dead reckoning, to use [DF radio fixes] along with all the other available methods, to establish a well-considered compromise between the various sorts of information at his disposal. In particular, the use of radio fixes should not take the place of recognition and observation of marks, when this is possible.*

You can't say better than that.

Merchant shipping and warships are still required to carry RDF equipment. This is largely because the equipment has a couple of SOS frequencies (500 and 2182 kHz) which enable the rescue services to home in on the transmitter. Helicopters and boats designed for rescue at sea also use VHF direction finders to find any vessel transmitting a MAYDAY message. The vessel can be positioned with considerable accuracy when two stations receive the signal at the same time.

Computer-aided navigation (CAN)

Merchant shipping has used computers on board for many years. Computers have gradually made their way on to pleasure yachts over the last few years, and are becoming every more popular as prices fall. Sooner or later, any cruising sailor can expect to encounter a computer on board.

Until the advent of on-board computers, every navigation system worked in fundamentally the same way: either the navigator homed in on signals from one or more fixed transmitters, or took a fix on three marks. The old Consol system used radio transmitters which sent a signal varying according to the direction from which it was received. RDF beacons transmit a signal which is picked up by means of a ferrite aerial; and Decca and Loran C work by allowing the receiver to locate the vessel at the intersection of two hyperbolic position lines.

Today's latest systems (Satnav and GPS) use satellites rather than earth-based transmitters, but they use the same logic. On the basis of one or two transmissions, the computer can work out where the boat is. The major difference (though Decca and Loran C have also recently been updated) is that the latest systems can:

- ■ automatically receive the signals;
- ■ analyse the signals without manual intervention;
- ▣ calculate the results in seconds;
- ■ give an idea of the reliability of the results on the basis of signal quality;
- ■ integrate their results with data from on-board measuring equipment (log, compass, anemometer) to work out current and angle of leeway;
- ■ retrace the route to a precise point using the 'man overboard' function;
- ■ plot a course on an electronic chart.

In the following pages we shall take a look at the four main navigational systems available to the recreational sailor. Decca and Loran C are quite likely to be supplanted over time by satellite systems, particularly GPS, which offers such substantial advantages. We also need to touch on radar as part of our equipment 'strategy'. Radar does not work in the same manner as the other systems, but it is an excellent tool for working out one's position relative to other boats or the coast.

Radar

In the past only professional seafarers used radar, but technical progress has brought it within the reach of the leisure sailor or motor vessel user, for a reasonable price. Modern screens can be used in full or semi-daylight. The common perception of radar is as a method for seeing over a distance; in fact it carries only about 10% further than the eye can see; but it comes into its own at night and in conditions of reduced visibility. Radar is thus a particularly useful coastal navigation tool and an invaluable safety aid in fog or in heavy traffic.

Principle

Radar functions simply on echoes. It transmits electromagnetic signals; any signal which encounters an obstacle is reflected back and seen as an echo on the screen. Radar waves travel at 300,000km per second, and the machine uses the delay between transmission and reception to estimate the distance to the reflecting object.

The antenna turns in a full circle, so the screen shows a picture of the complete surroundings of the boat. You can see the outline of the coast, landmarks and other boats, take relative bearings and tell how far these objects are from your vessel. This allows you in turn to

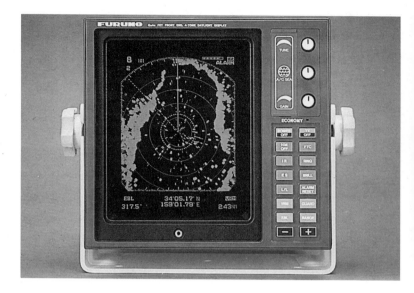

reckon your own position, and to tell whether there is any danger of collision with a moving object.

Accuracy

The radar is good at spotting high, hard, angular objects like the cliffs at Dover or a supertanker. It is less good on soft, low, round or absorbent objects which echo less well, such as mud banks, sandy beaches or small fibreglass boats.

For this reason, you should systematically doubt radar pictures when you are using them to make a landfall. Take into account the type of coastline you are approaching. It will look different on the screen from the chart. A tree which your almanac thinks is an excellent marker will be indistinct or invisible on the radar. All small sailing vessels should carry a masthead radar reflector for this reason. Atmospheric disturbance (rain, snow or hail) and large waves clutter up the radar image considerably, and can be suppressed to some extent by using anti-clutter controls on the set.

Operations

Cruising radars are easy to use, and the novice user will quickly master the set with the help of the manufacturer's manual. In outline, the following will be the procedure:

1 All adjustments to zero, apart from the tuning. Range at 4 or 8 miles.

2 Switch to standby to warm the set up.

3 When the 'ready' light comes on, switch on. The aerial begins to turn. (On modern radars steps 2 and 3 may be taken together.)

4 Adjust screen brightness to see the aerial trace.

■

Short radar glossary

ACR: anti-clutter rain

ACS: anti-clutter sea

BRILL: brilliance (luminosity adjustment, like the brightness control on a television)

CPA: closest point of approach (estimates proximity of passage to a point)

EBL: electronic bearing line (position line, or bearing if attached to a compass)

FTC: fast time constant (reduces rain echo)

GAIN: (adjusts signal amplification according to signal strength)

HM OFF: heading marker off (suppresses orientation line showing centre line of boat, useful if viewing weak echoes dead ahead)

HUD: head up display

IRS: interference rejection system (cuts down interference from other radars)

NUD: north up display (requires gyroscopic compass to work)

PL: pulse length

PRR: pulse repetition rate (800–3200 Hz depending on distance selected)

RACON: buoy fitted with radar reflector

RAMARK: radar or radio beacon transmitting on radar frequencies

RANGE: (adjustable)

RING: (brings up concentric circles on screen)

RM: relative motion (use with CPA for checking how vessels are moving relative to yours)

ST-BY: stand by (set does not transmit, but remains switched on)

STC: sensitivity time control (reduces sea echo)

TM: true motion (actually shows your vessel moving across the screen); useful for landfalls because the land stays still, but causes collision avoidance problems

TUNE: receiver tuning

VRM: variable range marker (gives precise distance to an echo or point; used repeatedly, this allows you to make position circles for your boat)

5 Turn up the gain gradually until you can see echoes or sea interference.

6 Adjust tuning as required to improve the picture.

7 Move to your normal working range and adjust anti-clutters if necessary. Keep anti-clutter adjustments at the lowest level possible so as not to drown out weak echoes.

Satellite navigation

Principles

Currently, all devices use the four satellites that make up the Transit system, positioned in a polar orbit of about 1 hour 48 minutes, at 1,000km above the Earth's surface.

The ground stations program the satellites with the characteristics of the orbits that they will make, and the satellite then transmits the characteristics of the current orbit to the onboard receiver.

The onboard receiver compares the frequency of the satellite's signal with the reference frequency provided by the oscillator on the boat (about 400 mHz). The relative motion of the boat and the satellite create a variation in frequency (Doppler effect).

If the position of the satellite, the true course and the speed of the boat are known, then the device can calculate the position of the boat. At the time of writing, the US Navy is gradually changing over from Transit to GPS.

Operating instructions

A satellite can be used when its elevation over the horizon falls between 10° and 75°. Outside that bracket, the calculated position is unreliable. Recent units give the times during which the satellite will be passing overhead for the hours and days to come.

The unit should be switched on three-quarters of an hour before the satellite passes over, so that the reference frequency provided by the oscillator can have stabilised by the time the measurement is taken. Since the unit draws quite a lot of current, it is best to keep the machine on standby, where only the oscillator is drawing power.

At full power, which requires quite a good power supply to provide the 10 to 30 watts necessary, the dead reckoning can be kept up to date as the satellites pass overhead (every 90 minutes at moderate latitudes), provided that the satellite navigation system is linked in with the log and the ship's compass.

Accuracy

In principle, the system is accurate to within a tenth of a nautical mile, plus 0·2 nautical miles per knot of error in the speed of the boat – which mounts up in a multi-hulled boat going at 20 knots. In practice, expect an accuracy of within half a nautical mile.

■

Auxiliary functions for radioelectrical navigation systems

Way points: Anything between 4 and 30 way points can be entered into the memory, according to the capacity, which then breaks the route to be followed into stages. One function allows the distance and heading of the next way point to be permanently displayed, and when that one is reached, the next one comes up on the screen. This is the ideal system for lazy navigators.

Orthodromic-loxodromic routes: An additional refinement which allows you to switch between displays giving the orthodromic and loxodromic routes, along with the distance and heading in each case. Pretty useful! Without this clever little gadget, it can take a good quarter of an hour to calculate the orthodromic route.

Man overboard: By pressing a button, possibly linked to the cockpit, the point at which the person falls overboard is memorised. As far as the unit is concerned, it's just another way point, and it then displays the distance and heading back to the point in question. Marvellous, but still not a reason to do without your safety harness.

Auxiliary functions

This type of navigational apparatus also tells the time, accurate to within 1 second, which can be very useful for navigating by the stars, but only when the Satnav breaks down. The other auxiliary functions are the calculation of way points, comparison of heading and distance for both orthodromic and loxodromic routes, along with a 'man overboard' function (for details, see the boxed section).

GPS satellite system.

GPS

The Global Positioning System uses a new network of 24 American satellites which are in high orbit (20,000km or so above the Earth) and travelling round the Earth every 12 hours. It allows you to position the boat 24 hours a day (unlike Transit) and wherever you are on the globe.

131

20,000km.

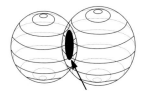

The transmissions from two satellites show that your position must be somewhere on this circle.

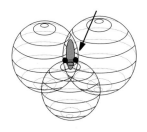

When you receive three signals, you know you must be at one of these two points. The uncertainty is displayed by your GPS kit.

Principle

Each satellite is constantly transmitting its own recognition code. The GPS reads the code and calculates the time taken for the code to reach it.

The machine knows the time and speed of signal transmission (the speed of light) and calculates its distance from the transmitter. The operation is carried out simultaneously on three satellites and gives a geographic position in two dimensions (longitude and latitude). It also works in three dimensions, reading four satellite transmissions and giving longitude, latitude and altitude of your position.

Operation

Apart from its precision, the great advantage of GPS is that it updates your position every 5 seconds. Some models can receive on multiple channels, thus reducing the time taken to find signals. Some older models required initialisation before they would work, but the latest types initialise themselves automatically.

Accuracy

The GPS is used for military purposes, so there are two grades of accuracy available. The satellites actually transmit two types of signals: the P (precise, or protected) code is used for military purposes, while the C/A code (clear acquisition) is for civilian use. The system is managed by the US army from Colorado Springs, which could shut down the signals for strategic reasons. Apart from that, a number of outside influences can upset it.

■ The satellites transmit information of varying quality. Nevertheless, the ground station in America corrects any anomaly in the orbiting path when the satellite passes overhead, by changing its transmission message. The high-altitude orbits used are in any case extremely stable.

■ The satellites used for the calculation may be poorly positioned relative to one another. Just like landmarks used for position lines, they should not be too close together or too far apart. The ideal angle is 60°.

■ The receiver aerial may be badly positioned or poorly maintained.

Despite all these things that can go wrong, the GPS user can expect to have a position to within about 25m (in other words, exceptionally precise!). The Pentagon would never let things get so bad as to allow errors of 100m (and which of us would worry if they did?).

Auxiliary functions

Most GPS sets are not content to tell you where you are. They can extrapolate between two points and tell you your speed, heading, time and any deviation from the route you have said you want to follow. They will also record way points which allow you to correct your own navigation for your destination.

The most sophisticated sets may be hooked up to other gadgets like chart readers and autopilots.

Decca

Principle

The old units are used in conjunction with special charts on which hyperbolas of different colours are printed according to the station in question. The numbers of the hyperbolas and their colour are marked on the unit. The position of the boat was read from the intersection of the different coloured hyperbolas marked on the unit. Newer equipment gives the position directly in geographical co-ordinates. Coverage is excellent for the Channel and the North Sea, and good for the eastern Atlantic, with the exception of a couple of gaps in the Bay of Biscay. In the Mediterranean, it is better to use Loran.

Operation

Very simple for the current models. They require relatively little power (less than 10 watts), and so can be left switched on permanently. The estimated position is entered at departure, to the nearest 15 nautical miles (usually rather better when starting from a port). All you have to do then is to read the position from the display. The machine makes new fixes several times a minute.

Accuracy

To within anything between 0·1 nautical miles and 200m, depending on the distance of the boat from the transmitter. The better units even give the estimated error.

Auxiliary functions

With more advanced units, it is also possible to keep the DR up to date by interfacing them with the log and the compass. Way points and man overboard functions are also available.

Loran C

Principle

'Long Range Navigation C' is a hyperbolic system similar to Decca. As with the latter, the older units require the position to be plotted on special charts, over which the Loran C hyperbolas have been super-imposed. Current models give geographical co-ordinates. The area covered extends as far as the coast of the Americas, the Far East and the Mediterranean.

Operation

Switch it on, let it warm up, and then enter the code of the station you want. When on automatic, the unit takes care of all this itself.

Accuracy

A quarter of a nautical mile during the day, half a mile at night. Accuracy varies considerably depending on how far away the transmitter is.

Auxiliary functions

Updating of the DR via interface with log and compass, way points and man overboard.

CAN: advice and usage

It would be absurd to rely blindly on CAN equipment, however precise the readouts it gives. They are not quite 100% reliable and you do not want to be the victim of someone else's breakdown. Alongside this equipment, you need to use your own calculations, made in the age-old way, and compare the results. In coastal navigation it is easy to check the accuracy of their information. A bearing taken on one or two identifiable landmarks will give you a good confirmation; in the same way, the depth sounder will often confirm or deny the position you have been given.

■ Never stop watching the landscape around you. Your instruments will give you a position, but this must be checked against the coastal profile, buoys and landmarks around you.

■ One of the most useful functions of a positioning system for coastal navigation is tracing way points. If you need to pass round a certain buoy, for instance, in order to pass some danger spot, you can input the question of the buoy and then let the instrument tell you the course required to sail for it. This is a particularly useful function for cruiser racing, when you need to find an offshore mark.

Offshore, satellite positioning systems may be used in the same way as sextant and stars used to be. Taking one or two positions in the course of the day should be enough. There is no point running your battery down for the fun of it. You should keep a back-up, though, in the form of dead-reckoning based on log, compass, leeway and currents. You might even get the sextant out of its box!

Meeting merchant ships and ferries

To round off this survey of the various ways of establishing your position at sea, we must mention one method that is slightly more unorthodox, but very effective: taking bearings on the courses followed by any large merchant ships that you might meet. The appearance of a ship on the horizon should not be considered as unusual or a matter of chance. These ships follow lanes whose overall pattern is as precisely laid out as a railway network, with main lines, branch lines and junctions.

By taking the bearing of the merchant ship's course, it is usually possible to work out its destination which consequently provides a valuable indication of one's own position.

The main cargo routes are well known, and the most important ones are to be found on the Pilot book charts. On the East Atlantic, there is Ushant-Cape Finisterre; on the French side of the English Channel, there is Ushant-les Casquets-la Bassurelle; on the English side: Bishop Rock (Scilly)-Lizard-Start Point-Royal Sovereign. These routes are the seagoing equivalent of motorways, with traffic going off in different directions at junctions, marked on the charts by pink lines about two miles wide.

Other less important routes can easily be deduced from the course of the ship that is met: often all that is needed is to lay the protractor-ruler on the chart, along the bearing of the course followed. The Pilot books also describe the activity of merchant shipping in the various ports, and consequently the sort of ship that will be using them. It is easy to learn the difference between a banana boat (white and heading for Dieppe), a ship carrying ore (black and maybe coming from Cardiff), and a warship in its dapper grey paintwork, coming and going pretty much as it pleases.

To get an accurate bearing of the merchant ship's course, the best thing is to wait for the moment when you cross its track, and its masts come into line with each other. If you are not crossing its track, a real bearing cannot be taken, but at least it can be estimated, and that is often good enough.

Traffic separation schemes

1. The use of lanes

This is compulsory. However, a boat may choose to avoid them and either

■ pass outside the lanes, leaving a good distance between itself and the lane; or

■ use the coastal navigation zone (between the lane and the land).

The skipper of the vessel has the responsibility for making the choice on the basis of the relative safety offered by each option.

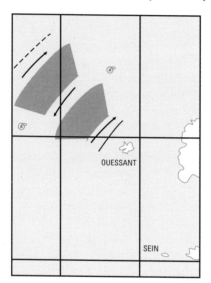

2. Within a scheme

All vessels must follow the general direction of traffic flow within their lane. They must manoeuvre to avoid collisions, in accordance with the International Regulations for Prevention of Collisions at Sea.

It is prudent to:

■ avoid any sudden change of course;

■ keep your distance from other vessels by using the entire width of the lane;

■ avoid sailing along the edges of lanes and separation zones.

3. Entering and leaving a lane

Vessels are normally expected to enter and leave shipping lanes at the lane ends.

They may, if necessary:

■ enter from the side of a lane if they are travelling in the same direction as traffic in that lane;

■ leave by the side of a lane, but at the smallest angle practicable.

4. Crossing a lane

A vessel may cross a lane or both lanes, but must do so at right angles to the general direction of the traffic in the lane or lanes.

The following rules apply:

■ in a shipping lane, fishing vessels, vessels of less than 20m in length and sailing vessels must not obstruct the passage of shipping;

■ in the separation zone, fishing is permitted, but other traffic is prohibited except in case of emergency or if cutting across the separation scheme.

The routes used by ferries are also followed very precisely. On some of them, the traffic is so intense that the problem is not so much of knowing where you are, but rather knowing where to pass to avoid them all. The Straits of Dover are well marked from that point of view.

■

One of our boats was on its way back to France from England but did not trust its dead-reckoning. It called up Ushant Traffic (which monitors the western approaches to the English Channel for merchant shipping) on VHF channel 11 and gave them the names of two merchant ships it had recently seen. Ushant Traffic was then able to identify our boat on the radar screen and give it a precise position. The duty watch then kept an eye on the boat all the way until it was safely anchored at the Stiff.

Landfall

The first member of the crew to sight land has the right to a double Scotch, and that is a rule never to be forgotten. However, then comes the important job of actually making your landfall. This means that the land you have spotted must be identified, and the boat's position in relation to it fixed before proceeding on to harbour.

If you can, choose an area and a time for your landfall. The ideal is a sheer coastline, with prominent landmarks or profile, approached over a shoaling bottom with characteristic features (like the Bancs de Sable off Paimpol in Brittany).

The ideal time is towards dawn: it is easy to establish position by the powerful lighthouses and enter harbour very early. Even if neither of these ideal conditions is fulfilled, other aids are available: positions can be transferred, soundings taken, a radio fix taken, or merchant ships spotted. As a last resort, candles could be lit to your patron saint.

However, the important thing is to examine scrupulously all the available information, ensuring that there is nothing contradictory, and that all the facts agree. If something isn't quite right then don't try to land come what may, but instead try to find some additional information, keeping a safe distance until you have an idea of what is going on. There are even times when you have to know how to give up the idea of making a landfall, when you know – either by experience, or by information gathered – that it is going to be difficult to enter a port at a given time. After all, is life on shore so wonderful that you are ready to take all sorts of silly risks to get there?

In practice, there is no general advice for making a landfall: they are all quite different and they can even be quite emotional occasions, depending on the sort of crossing that has just been made. For the navigator, it is the moment of truth, when the validity of the dead reckoning is put to the test. Up until that time, there has always been a margin of uncertainty in the navigation, and it is possible that some slight error may have crept in and upset the calculations. Landfalls always contain a potential for the unexpected, and this is part of their fascination.

It is always better to check everything three times than to check it only once and wreck the boat.

Communications

We now pass on to maritime communications, which are an increasingly integrated part of navigation and of safety at sea, since they are an important link in any rescue operation.

We have no intention of summarising the contents of a dozen electronics catalogues, with portable telephones and onboard telex machines; nor shall we waste our time on satellite communication systems which are for navigators in a hurry, not for cruising sailors. Similarly, we shall not spend time on the SSB (single-side band) system which is used by offshore sailors and professionals. We shall limit our survey to VHF radios, which are widespread and affordable.

VHF is the most widely used method of marine communication. Harbour authorities, coastal stations, lighthouses and most other vessels have a VHF set. You can thus easily get a weather report from a signal station, reserve a marina space with a harbourmaster, contact the bridge officer on a tanker, or (as a last resort) call for help on channel 16. In addition, if you have two-way VHF set (call select), you can use the radio to make telephone calls through a coastal station. The VHF band covers the 156 to 162 mHz frequencies, and the average transceiver, if it has the right aerial placed sufficiently high up, can manage a range of about 50 miles.

VHF use is subject to certain restrictions:

■ the set needs to be approved by the DTI Marine Licensing section, Waterloo Bridge House, Waterloo Road, London SE1 8UA;

■ the user needs to have passed an exam set by the RYA (see their booklet G26);

■ the set will need an annual inspection, which requires the payment of a small licence fee.

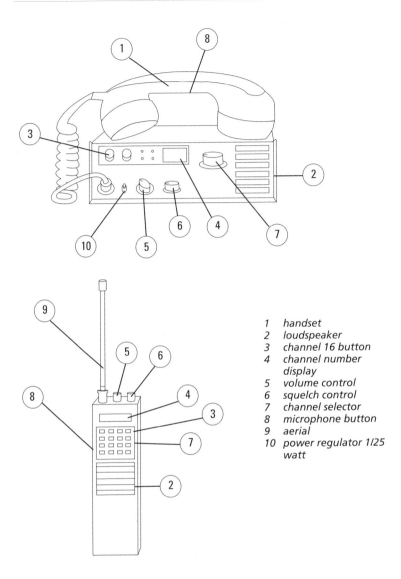

1   handset
2   loudspeaker
3   channel 16 button
4   channel number
    display
5   volume control
6   squelch control
7   channel selector
8   microphone button
9   aerial
10 power regulator 1/25
    watt

Where and when to use VHF

Safety Channel 16 is reserved for safety-related traffic. This is the channel used for distress calls and requests for assistance. The RNLI, coastal radio stations and all ships monitor channel 16 constantly.

Weather
The coastal stations broadcast the weather forecast at regular intervals. You will often find, if you miss the shipping forecast, that a coast radio operator will be kind enough to repeat the relevant parts for you.

Contacting professional sea users

Fishing vessels, harbour authorities, commercial freighters etc, all work with a VHF set constantly on. Every profession has its own habitual channel for conversations: thus you will usually find the harbour authorities on 9, fishing vessels on a different channel depending on their home port, and so on.

Boat to boat communications

Any boat equipped with a VHF set can talk to any other similarly equipped boat on a ship to ship channel reserved for this purpose.

Using the public telephone network

A coastal station will be able to connect you to the domestic and international telephone system. You can call up anyone you like!

Telephone calls in the other direction, from land to sea, are not possible with a one-way set. Two-way VHF sets using automatic maritime radio exchanges may be called up without even going through the operator.

How to use VHF

Using the equipment is very simple. There are four basic buttons on all sets, from the most basic to the most sophisticated:

■ on-off: this is generally incorporated with the volume control. In standby mode VHF sets use very little current;

■ transmit button: since the transmission and reception are on the same frequency, you cannot talk and listen at the same time; you need to punctuate your conversation with the phrases 'over' and 'message received';

■ channel select button: you can flick through the channels to find your chosen frequency;

■ squelch control: this cuts down interference.

VHF: the ten commandments

1   Use VHF only for essential conversations, so as not to clog up the airwaves.

2   Use a channel only for its intended purpose.

3   Before you transmit, ensure that others are not using the same channel.

4   Name the vessel you are calling before identifying yourself, thus: 'Sereine, Sereine, this is Triagoz calling'.

5   Use the international code (listed overleaf) to spell out proper names.

6   Channel 16 is reserved for safety matters and for making first contact.

7 Any call on channel 16 which is not related to safety should be brief and followed by a move on to a working channel. Make sure that your listener understands your intended working channel, thus: 'Going to channel 6' or 'Going to channel 72, that is seven two'.

8 When possible, for conversations between boats use channels 6, 8, 72 and 77 as working channels.

9 Use reduced-power transmission when possible.

10 In tricky waters, such as approaching a narrow harbour mouth or when crossing traffic separation lanes, monitor channel 16.

The international alphabet

letter	code	letter	code
A	Alpha	T	Tango
B	Bravo	U	Uniform
C	Charlie	V	Victor
D	Delta	W	Whiskey
E	Echo	X	X-ray
F	Foxtrot	Y	Yankee
G	Golf	Z	Zulu
H	Hotel	0	Nadazero
I	India	1	Unaone
J	Juliet	2	Bissotwo
K	Kilo	3	Terrathree
L	Lima	4	Kartefour
M	Mike	5	Pantafive
N	November	6	Soxisix
O	Oscar	7	Setteseven
P	Papa	8	Oktoeight
Q	Quebec	9	Novenine
R	Romeo	point	decimal
S	Sierra	full stop	stop

5

PASSAGE
MAKING

You can choose any route you like at sea. All the reference points and documents, along with the various techniques that allow you to find your position, are there to give you the means to exploit that basic freedom. There is no fixed way of getting from A to B: the route can be chosen according to circumstances and taste.

As for taste, well, chacun à son goût, as the French say – there's no saying any route is better than any other from that point of view. Some people just spend all their time wandering along; others want to have a comfortable life and therefore choose routes that take them out of the way of all harsh encounters with the elements, and others like speed. There are realists and dreamers, old-fashioned sea dogs and modernists with every sort of technological aid, people going to the Scilly Islands and people going to Lyonesse. Mood influences the choice of route greatly, and gives it a certain colour.

However, there are the particular circumstances of the journey that must also be taken into account. Even once the leg has been chosen and the distance that has to be covered calculated, the route still remains to be finalised. The wind direction can make all the difference: the trip can either be a short one, or become absolutely interminable. In fact, the route is rarely defined in terms of distance, but rather more often in terms of time. A route is a certain number of days and hours spent at sea in constantly changing conditions: the water level rises and falls; the tidal stream changes direction. The wind rises, drops or turns, the sea can be choppy here and calm there, the sun is either to your back or in your eyes, fog can come and night can fall.

Whatever the state of mind of the sailor, all these circumstances demand minute preparation: any route can be chosen, but not all are either possible or reasonable. In other words, the first task is to make sure that the route chosen is safe. After that we can talk about the fine details.

Choosing a route

It is very rare to come back from a sea voyage without having learnt anything new. Every route always has something unknown and unexpected about it – there is even an element of risk. Choosing a safe route does not eliminate all possible risks. but it does allow you to foresee as much as possible.

There are various sorts of data to be considered. Some are permanent and given by either the charts or the Pilot books: these can be the characteristics of the area to be crossed, with the various blackspots that need to be avoided, with sudden shallows, isolated dangers, difficult channels or shipping lanes. Reference points must also be taken into account: beacons, landmarks, lights and radio signals. There are other factors that are variable in nature, but predictable, such as the tides, which can make certain routes impassable at certain times. Others are predictable to a certain extent, such as the wind, visibility, sea conditions in particular places. The rest are unforeseeable: sudden changes in the weather, problems with equipment, human error, hidden beacons and buoys adrift.

Choosing a route means facing up to all these factors and seeing how the overall picture shapes up. The order in which they have to be examined cannot be systematised, since one of them will be of predominant importance according to the sort of circumstances you are dealing with. Sometimes there are numerous routes available. Sometimes a route suggests itself fairly readily, but you have to make sure that there is an alternative in case of difficulty.

So much for theory, here are some examples.

From la Vilaine to le Palais

We suggest you read this section with a chart (SHOM 7033 P) and parallel rules or protractor beside you.

We are at Tréhiguier, in the mouth of la Vilaine. The next stop is at le Palais, on Belle-Île.

The direct route shows a variety of problems. There is a shallow (the shelf at la Recherche) then a large obstacle (the line of rock jutting out from the headland at Quiberon, with the island of Houat right in the middle). Should we steer a course round la Recherche or not? Everything depends on the weather and the route that we choose in order to cross the reef. There are three possible ways over the reef: la Teignouse, le Béniguet, les Soeurs. There is also a fourth solution, which is to go round the Grands-Cardinaux; this is referred to in the Pilot as the eastern passage.

Whichever passage we take, the distance varies very little: 28·5 nautical miles by le Béniguet, 29·5 nautical miles by la Teignouse and by les Soeurs, 30·5 nautical miles by the Grands-Cardinaux.

First choice

The weather is good and seems unlikely to change. There is a steady NE wind, the visibility is good. The boat will probably make 6kn. The trip will probably take about 5 hours.

With these winds, the sea won't be too bad over la Recherche,

The Béniguet passage, NW of Houat

and we will be able to cross it as long as we keep a pilot's foot of 2m.

Since the route by le Béniguet is the shortest, we will look at this one first of all. With these winds, the passage will be easy. The only problem is that it isn't lit and so we can't do it at night.

The route by les Soeurs seems a little less simple: the landmarks are a good way away, and so there is some danger of confusion. Again, it would be impossible to sail it by night.

La Teignouse can be sailed either day or night, as can the eastern passage. Should we take account of the tide? The currents are relatively strong in all the channels (except for the eastern passage) and it is best to go through as the tide is falling. The best time to set out is high water, and we will have the current behind us throughout the trip.

All in all, there is a lot to choose from. There don't seem to be any traps or pitfalls and we can always find a port to leeward: either Houat or le Palais. The only precaution that needs to be taken is if we are passing either by le Béniguet or la Teignouse: we should take care not to sail too close to Houat or the reef at Béniguet, where we could be in trouble if there is any kind of mishap.

Second choice

This time the wind is fresh from the west and the visibility is less good. At 5kn (which will give us about 3 nautical miles per hour into the wind) we estimate that the trip will take us 10 hours whatever route we take. If the course is dead into the wind, then by taking the beat into account, the four routes come out about the same.

In this weather, the sea will probably be rather heavy on la Recherche, and it would be better to avoid it. In the passes over the

147

reef, the sea will be dreadful right through the ebb tide, when the tide will be flowing in the opposite direction to the wind. Would it be better to pass over during the flood? It is not yet certain that we would be able to get over, beating against the current. The only time it seems possible is either at high or low water.

Advantages and disadvantages of the different routes

■ La Teignouse: the passage is wide enough for us to be able to tack on the way through, and we would be sheltered from the reef during most of the trip.

■ Le Béniguet: the passage is short, but too narrow for beating: if the wind is west we can go through fast, but if it drops we'll be stuck.

■ Les Soeurs: again, we would get little shelter from the reef. The passage itself is long and narrow and the landmarks would be difficult to identify – this is probably not a safe route to take.

■ The eastern passage: here the current is not as strong as elsewhere, and if we passed the Grands-Cardinaux at a safe distance, in 30m of water, the sea would probably not be as bad as elsewhere, and we would be able to tack. The problem is that once past the Grands-Cardinaux, we would have no shelter. Furthermore, at night, if visibility was poor, we would have only one light from the Cardinaux.

What time should we then get under way in order to pass over the reef at the right time? Leaving la Vilaine during the flood is out of the question. If we left at high water, then we would miss low water at le Béniguet and la Teignouse. We must therefore get under way at the end of the ebb tide in order to be able to pass over at high water. If we choose the eastern passage, then the choice becomes more simple: we can go round at any time, as long as we give the Cardinaux a wide berth. The best option seems to be to leave Tréhiguier at high water, in order to go through the passage at the end of the ebb.

What options do we have if things don't go to plan? As long as we are in Quiberon bay we can always turn back up into la Vilaine. If anything strange happens around la Teignouse. then we have on our lee either Houat, Port-Navalo or la Trinité. On the route around the eastern passage, we could bear off either towards la Turballe or le Croisic. It is possible to get into any of these ports at any hour of the tide.

If we need an extra option coming out of either la Teignouse or le Béniguet, then we could be in difficulties, since we would have to be well out of any of the channels before we could let ourselves turn towards the SE. In fact, we could always turn right round. All the same it would be better not to go through le Béniguet at the end of the day, because going back through it at night would be lunacy.

Only one last question has to be taken into account, which would be of decisive importance if the visibility were bad: what is there that would allow us to keep an eye on the course we were steering? It would be very difficult to find the entrance to la Teignouse in the murk, and even finding the entry to le Béniguet would not be easy. The only reasonable route is therefore the one that avoids all the dangers, that is the eastern passage. We can make the entire trip navigating by dead reckoning, and then make landfall on Kerdonis point which has no outlying dangers and is easy to spot.

All in all, given the weather conditions, the eastern passage is the safest. The routes passing by either les Soeurs or le Béniguet are rather perilous. The route passing by la Teignouse is good only if there is sufficient visibility. However, the weather can change. If we were to find ourselves towards the end of a depression and find that the wind picked up from the NW and the visibility improved, then we could look at things in a different light: the route passing through la Teignouse would be the shortest, and as soon as we cleared the passage we could head for le Palais with the wind abaft the beam.

On the other hand, if we passed round the Grands-Cardinaux, then we would have to continue to beat for a long time, which would be tiring, the route would not be so safe, and the journey would certainly take longer. Then again, if the wind were to drop from the SW, then the eastern passage would be the best solution. We would still need to be able to see when the wind was going to turn, wonder whether it was going to change in force, and what the sea would be like as a result.

From Concarneau to Royan

It is 185 nautical miles from Concarneau to Royan. The route can be plotted as a straight line, going outside the island group: Groix, Belle-Île, Noirmoutier, Ré and Oléron. It is the sort of trip that a boat suitable for coastal navigation can do very easily – a Glénans 7·60, for example, which does 5·5kn in a good wind, would do it in 34 hours.

However, Mousquetaires are not built for the high seas, and therefore we will need to be able to find harbours of refuge that we can get to quickly if the weather starts to deteriorate, or if we simply have to give up the idea of getting to the planned destination.

Using the chart and the Pilot, we draw up a list of ports that would be easy enough to get to if we had to, which are well marked, accessible at any hour of the tide, both during the day and at night, and which would give shelter from winds coming in off the sea.

Starting from Concarneau, we find Port-Tudy on Groix, Sauzon and le Palais on Belle-Île, then le Croisic, Pornic, le Bois-de-la-Chaize on Noirmoutier, Port-Joinville in the island of Yeu, les Sables d'Olonne, Ars-en-Ré. There is also shelter to be had at le Pertuis

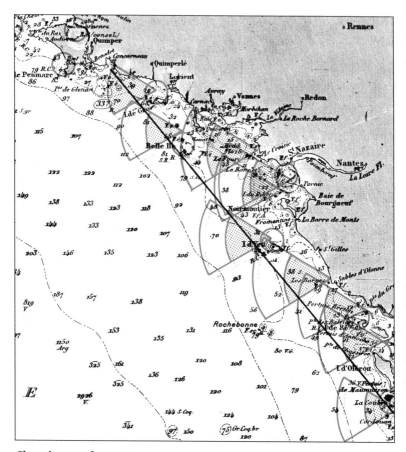

Choosing a safe route

This includes choosing your emergency exit. If we wanted to take a Glénans 7·60 from Concarneau to Royan, for example, we should have to be sure that there was shelter from the wind available all along the coast in the event of an accident or bad weather from the west.

There is a safe area of about 60° in front of each refuge (a Glénans 7·60, even when disabled, can still sail with the wind up to about 30° on the weather quarter), this safe area stretching out to 20 nautical miles in front of the port (the shaded areas mark where the boat would be less than four hours from port), even up to about 30 nautical miles from port (the white areas show zones from where you can make port in about 6 hours).

There are three blank spots on the way. These are periods when the boat would not be in easy reach of shelter: between Groix and Belle-Île, to windward of Belle-Île and between Chassiron and Royan. Each of these blanks will have to be faced up to differently, depending on local conditions. (Chart of the SHOM.)

d'Antioche (either in la Rochelle or the island of Aix-Château d'Oleron) and, last of all, there is Royan. Is this enough ports to give us easy access to shelter at any point along the route?

If the weather forecast warns us that conditions are going to get worse, then we have to be able to make port in 3-4 hours, 6 at the outside. We would have to take the possibility of some sort of accident into account, which would mean that the boat would be less manoeuvrable. (In the worst possible case, it is possible to sail with a jury rig with the wind up to 30° on the quarter.)

Under these conditions, in the area of each port, there is a safe sector which can be plotted on the chart. We see that the direct route from Concarneau to Royan is not entirely covered by these safe areas. There are a few blanks that we shall have to look at closely.

The first of these comes straight after Groix: between Lorient and Quiberon there is no shelter along the coast. If the weather is good we can make the trip without worrying too much. However, if the weather is not so good, then it would be a good idea to modify the route a little to place oneself as fast as possible in the safe sector after that stretch, which would be the port of Sauzon.

After les Poulains point, there is another blank: we pass the wild coast of Belle-Île. This is very pretty, but not much use in a storm. Even in good weather, it's best to give it a decent berth so as to leave a little room to play with on either side in case there is any problem with the boat. If the forecast is not so good, then it would be better to leave the route and pass directly downwind of the island.

If we pass to windward, then we will be out of safe areas right up to the mouth of the Loire. However, this is a bit of a special case: we're just a little far away from shelter, which is only a problem if the weather is really bad. At all events, we would soon be in the safe area for the island of Yeu, followed immediately by that of les Sables-d'Olonne: it is very clear from this that passing the island of Yeu to leeward would not be a good idea, because we would then be windward of a stretch of coast without any possible shelter.

One blank remains, which is the most serious: between Chassiron point and Royan. Here it is vital to pay attention to the weather forecasts. If the weather is going to be bad, then it is best to give up and make for le Pertuis d'Antioche, hoping that things will improve. If the weather is reasonable, then it is best to sail out to sea so as to get into the safe area before Royan as fast as possible.

All in all, once the areas have been plotted on the chart, there remain three blanks where there seem to be no alternative safe options: after Groix, to windward of Belle-Île, and to windward of Oléron. However, the drawing shows up a solution that would not have been apparent at first glance: in all of the three areas, the solution seems to be to move further out to sea rather than sail nearer into shore. This allows us to reach the next safe area more quickly.

Of course, this solution only works for the sort of boat we have chosen, that is to say a Glénans 7·60 or a boat of the same category. A smaller boat, a Corsaire for example, could not make the trip in a single go, whatever happened, and for this sort of craft, the problems would be entirely different: in order to make the passage from

151

Groix to Belle-Île, it would need good weather conditions – if not, the only option would be to wait. For a deep-water cruiser, on the other hand, it is often safest to be out to sea.

These few examples do not show all possible aspects of the problems involved in choosing a route. They simply show the basic principles behind a line of thinking that sometimes has to be pushed a lot farther than we have taken it here. We will therefore have to deal with some of the pitfalls that you might meet, born out of an unhappy mixture of weather and local conditions.

A bay that offers no shelter can be a trap when the wind gets up just so as to block the entrance: Porto bay and the mistral have mastered this trick perfectly. There is also the reef with the tide running towards it as the wind dies down – this can happen to the south of the Chaussée de Sein, and can be a very unpleasant experience. The channel with no leading marks (such as the one between Roches de Saint-Quay and the coast) can prove a problem if you have to beat and then night falls before the yacht is through. The Gaine channel (between les Héaux-de-Brehat and Tréguier) can cause problems, when you suddenly realise that the leading marks cannot be seen against the light on a lovely sunny evening. Other channels can become traps when fog drifts in. What is important to note in all this is that there is nothing baffling or unforeseeable about it all. In most cases, surprises can be avoided by paying attention to the weather forecast and thinking ahead.

To sum up, a safe route is the one that allows you a little room for manoeuvre, so that you can steer away from the dangers of the coast, allow for accidents or tiredness. This is the sort of margin that you should allow with obstacles too: always go about well before you have to (especially after a long tack) and change sail when necessary. The route you should take is the one suggested by the old French sailor's proverb, 'If you want to live long and hale, give wide berths and reduce your sail'.

A safe course is where you have both water to manoeuvre in and plenty of escape routes. It should also be, above all, lined with a good number of easily verifiable reference points. However, the most thorough study of the charts and the most perfect grasp of navigational techniques can be reduced to nothing if seasickness sets in, and tiredness can multiply the risks of an accident.

Improving on your course

Both comfort and speed can vary enormously over the same route. As for the former, there is not much to be said: if you want a quiet life, then you soon learn to avoid the open sea and to remember that islands and the coast can offer you some sheltered areas. Also, a course run with the wind free can be much more pleasant than a long hard beat to windward. If you've tried the latter, then you'll know what is meant by the expression 'battling in the teeth of the wind'.

A comfortable route is also often a safe route, since it allows the crew to save their strength.

Choosing a fast route can be a matter of mood at the time, but it can also be a matter of safety, too. Even if you have settled on the idea of a gentle meander, you should always be in a position to change to a faster course at any moment, so as to be able to get into harbour quickly when bad weather threatens, for example. Going faster can also extend a boat's range: if you gain an hour here and there on a two-week cruise, then you might have time to fit in an extra port of call, which might turn out to be the best part of the trip.

Going fast is also what ocean-racing is all about. Speed is a controversial question in yachting, and opinions seem to fall into two camps. John Illingworth, the famous ocean racer, writes, 'Sailing a boat in an ocean race means driving it at its maximum speed in all weather encountered'. Hilaire Belloc, an old sea salt, whose work is perhaps not as well known as it should be, counters that 'from one's boat (at least from one which is a true companion) one must expect rational behaviour. One must say to oneself that, when she is making seven knots, she is doing well, and when she is making nine, she is upset and will be better for a night's rest'. These two quotations encapsulate remarkably well the two sides of an utterly fruitless, but passionately felt debate. Since it is hardly within the scope of this book to pursue the matter, let us simply refer those interested to John Illingworth's *Offshore* and Hilaire Belloc's *The Cruise of the Nona*.

Suffice it to say that there will come a day when you have had enough of trying to understand why people who have the same type of boat as you can seem to be going rather faster, why you are always badly placed when the wind changes and why you always make that bad tack in a strong tide. The time will come when you want to do better. This does not necessarily require you to have a competitive spirit, but is simply fascinating in itself. It is the challenge of proving yourself equal to that volatile trio of the sea, the wind and the tide – the three forces that make the choice of the fastest course an intriguing puzzle, set to try the ingenuity.

We shall try to lay out the principal rules and give an insight into some of the finer points.

The shortest route

At first sight. the direct course from A to B might seem the fastest. This is indeed often the case, and this is always the eventuality that has to be considered first, even when you know you are capable of devising and steering more complicated courses.

Sometimes, however, it is possible to get from A to B in less time by avoiding the direct route, especially when the wind, the tides and the sea conditions would mean that the boat was going rather more slowly on that route. We already know that it is best to avoid shallows in the interests of safety, but they must also be avoided if you want to sail fast. Shallow waters are likely to be short, steep and choppy, and can even bring the boat to a standstill. Flat water sailing is always faster.

It can also be good policy to move off the direct course in certain wind conditions, enabling you to side-step calm waters and seek a better wind. If you do this, then either the boat will go faster or you will be better able to get into position so that you can benefit from a change in the wind. Similarly, you might want to move off course to take advantage of a current that might help speed you up, or to offset the effects of a current that you are obliged to sail against.

At all events, the question is this: will the detour allow you to reach your destination faster than the course you had originally intended? The answer is not always an obvious one, far from it; indeed, if things are not carefully worked out in advance, you stand a good chance of losing time rather than gaining it.

The time that is lost avoiding shallows is hard to estimate. The real game begins when you change course because of the wind.

Wind strategy

It is easy to talk about avoiding areas of calm or areas where the wind is either too strong or too contrary, but it is much less easy to put it into practice. When the weather is fair and the breezes are fitful, the skill lies in being ready for the slightest breath of wind, and hanging onto it whatever happens. This can lead you off on some very strange detours. Spotting such things depends on acute observation; closer inshore, the art becomes more subtle still, and anyone who does not know the area well can very rapidly become completely bewildered.

In these cases, speculating on the wind can be rather a wild goose chase, and the various reference works are not always very helpful. There is nonetheless such a thing as wind psychology, not utterly fanciful, which Jacques Perret, a French specialist in navigation, has studied at some length. The chap maintains that the unity and lapse of time are one and the same thing (or something like that), but this is only really for those of you who believe that a copy of the complete works of Descartes is indispensable for proper navigation (hmm!).

Leaving such weighty matters aside, the use of coastal breezes requires the use of rather more readily accessible facts (but then, what do we mean by a fact anyway?). It is often worthwhile making detours to catch land breezes at night and sea breezes that rise in the afternoon when the gradient wind is particularly weak or in an unfavourable quarter. The problem is to know how far to go out to find them. This depends on the nature of the coastline and what the weather forecast predicts. The distance varies between 5 and 10 nautical miles, sometimes less, rarely more. You also have to think about coming inshore in time.

It is always hard to figure out what there is to be gained by going out of your way when the wind is weak. Covering twice the distance to get near land at night can be worthwhile if you are going to get the benefit of a good breeze throughout the night. On the other hand, it is infuriating to go inshore only to have the wind rise at sea. How do you know which is going to happen?

It is only possible to make predictions when the wind has become fairly settled, and even then the wind can still change direction. Before plunging into complicated calculations and navigational geometry, it is as well to keep up to date with the weather forecasts. Whatever plan you make is based on this information, and this is where the whole thing can become a game of chance.

What it amounts to is that there are considerable gains to be made in gambling with the wind, but that the gambles are only measurable in two basic kinds of situation:

■ when moving away from the direct course to get on a faster point of sailing;

■ to benefit from an expected change of wind.

Looking at things more closely, the second case is simply a variant on the first, and this is the one on which any decisions must be based. If you are to decide whether you will gain time by sailing faster along a longer course. you must first estimate the length of the detour, then the anticipated gain in speed as a result. and compare the two.

Estimating the longer course

In the diagram (right), it is evident that by moving away from the direct route, AB, by an angle a the distance to be covered is increased by a distance

By moving 10° from the direct route for three-quarters of the distance and then rejoining it for the last quarter at an angle of 30°, the first part of the journey is made 1.5% longer and the second part 15%, giving a total increase of 5%.

155

equalling mC + Cn. The value of this lengthening is naturally directly proportional to the angle a and the distance d, when one is still moving away from the original course.

First impressions are encouraging: in the present case, the increase in the distance to be covered seems to be fairly small. The calculations for different values of the angles a and b seem to confirm that impression:

for   5° :   0·4%   extra mileage
for 10° :   1·5%   extra mileage
for 15° :   3·5%   extra mileage
for 20° :   6·4%   extra mileage
for 25° : 10·0%   extra mileage
for 30° : 15·0%   extra mileage

All in all, it can be reckoned that anything up to a departure of 20° from the route does not add an unreasonable extra distance. Beyond that, the increase becomes more considerable, and the possible returns begin to diminish, unless the gain in speed is expected to be extraordinary.

Estimating the speed gained

In order to estimate the gain in speed with any degree of accuracy, you need to know the capabilities of your boat on all points of sailing and at different wind speeds. Clearly it is possible to get by with notional estimates, but you can acquire very precise knowledge for use on an occasion like this by taking the trouble to measure carefully the different speeds of the boat on the different points of sailing and drawing diagrams to illustrate how they compare.

Obviously, a polar diagram only works for the boat on which it is made, and for the conditions in which the measurements were taken (wind speed, sea, etc). The curves given opposite are only examples. They were made on a light displacement boat, 8m on the waterline (whose critical speed is therefore 2·4 x the square root of 8 = 6·8kn). They are nevertheless worth looking at, because they show up certain constants and characteristics shared with the majority of modern boats.

One of the curves was drawn up in rather brisk weather, the other in lighter conditions. The first fact to emerge is that the differences between points of sailing are much more marked in light than in heavier weather. This should go down in the book as rule one: **It is only worth making a detour to go faster in light weather: in heavy weather it is better to stay on the direct route unless some change is expected.**

The curve that emerges in light weather shows significant variation in speed in three sectors: when the wind is ahead, when it is astern and when it is abeam:

156

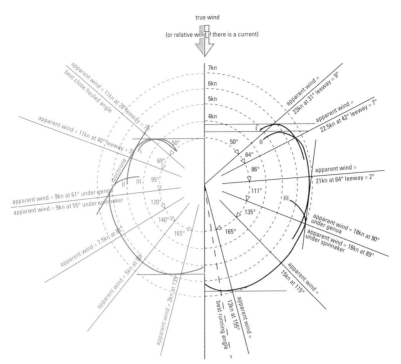

Speed diagrams Illustrating the performance of a boat 8m LWL (maximum displacement speed 6·8kn). In colour, diagram for a wind of 8kn. In black, diagram for a 19kn wind. Curve I: under jib; curve II: under genoa; curve III: under spinnaker.

■ With a headwind, the gap at the top of the diagram corresponds to the angle between tacks when sailing closehauled.

■ With the wind astern, it appears that the boat goes slightly faster when the wind is on one or the other quarter, which suggests that tacking downwind (ie wearing) may be useful.

■ With the wind abeam, the sudden acceleration noticed corresponds to the angle at which the spinnaker becomes more efficient than the genoa.

Between these sectors, the curve is more or less regular, and the speed varies little. From close fetch to close reach and from reach to broad reach, it is hard to see how a change in direction could lead to an increase in speed. Quite clearly, then, on these points of sailing, the direct course is the fastest. On the other hand, things are quite different in the three sectors where the speed varies. When the destination you are trying to reach is in the beam wind sector, could you run some of the distance under spinnaker on a broad reach, then finishing on a close reach? When the objective is to leeward, could you get there by two broad reaches rather than going straight for it dead downwind?

As far as the closehauled sector is concerned, the problem is clearly quite different.

157

■

Making a polar diagram

A polar diagram is the graphic representation of a boat's capabilities for a given strength of wind on the different points of sailing. To draw it, start from the centre of the diagram, marking out the vectors of a length proportional to the speed of the boat, according to the headings followed and in relation to the true wind. The polar curve joins the ends of all these vectors.

Measuring instruments

Some measuring instruments are needed to draw the diagram, but these do not need to be complicated pieces of electronic equipment: much more simple items will do the job perfectly adequately.

To measure the boat's heading relative to the true wind you use the steering compass.

To measure the leeway, you can make yourself a leeway meter. Take a school protractor with a large radius (say about 10cm), fix it to the transom, the round edge towards the stern and the straight edge at right angles to the axis of the boat. Fix a thin line about 10m long (fishing line will do) to the centre of the protractor and attach a 100-200g fishing weight to the end. The leeway is read off on the protractor.

To measure the speed, the Dutchman's log and the patent log are usually perfect since they serve the purpose better than electronic logs, which are too sensitive to momentary variations in speed.

To measure the wind speed, you need an anemometer: either handheld (not too expensive) or fixed to the mast head (quite pricey). A ventimeter is very cheap and can do the job quite well, the major drawback being that it only detects winds of over 6kn.

To measure the angle between the axis of the boat and the apparent wind, you need a wind vane, which must be at the mast head. This can be a wind sock such as you see in aerodromes or along motorways, or a sheet metal arrow like those you see on the tops of buildings. To get a good measurement of the angle, the support must have two arms on either side, adjusted at appropriate angles (60° and 40° to start with). If you're rich, you can allow yourself the luxury of the sort of electronic apparatus that combines anemometer and wind vane all in one.

Constructing the diagram

First you need to know the true wind. Its direction can be found either dead running or by taking the average of the headings followed when close-hauled on both tacks. Its speed is measured with wind astern by taking the sum of the apparent wind speed and that of the boat. If the apparent wind speed is too weak to be measured then don't worry, as this can be done later.

Next measure the speed and course of the boat for each point of sailing. Follow the heading on the compass, and, if necessary, correct it by the amount of leeway to obtain the true course of the boat. If the diagram is to

Here, progress can only be made by making a detour; and then it is only a question of working out which detour it is best to take. The diagram allows for the gain in speed for a given change of course to be reckoned precisely.

be realistic, a large number of measurements must be made: every 10 to 15° on a broad reach and on a reach: every 5° when reaching the limit of the spinnaker, and then the same when sailing from anywhere on a close reach to close-hauled.

While this is going on, measure the wind speed at least once. If you have a complete set-up, then note the speed and the apparent wind direction for each heading. If you only have a rudimentary wind vane, then measure the apparent wind speed for angles where its direction is easily identifiable (90°, 60°, 40°). As the apparent wind is much stronger at these points of sailing than with the wind astern, it's only with a dying wind that the ventimeter becomes inadequate.

You can then check the value of these measurements by making a simple diagram. Three curves are drawn: one with the spinnaker, another with the genoa, and a third with the jib. The three curves obtained for the same wind strength are all plotted on the same graph which, without hesitation, allows you to choose the best sail plan for a particular point of sailing and the most advantageous heading to steer.

NB. It is worthwhile (but not essential) to note the strength and direction of the apparent wind for several points of sailing on the diagram, since these are the only knowable factors against which performance can be established. When several diagrams have been drawn up for different strengths of wind, the arms of the wind vane can be adjusted for two very distinct points of sailing: for instance, the points when the spinnaker can be hoisted and when the genoa must be exchanged for the jib.

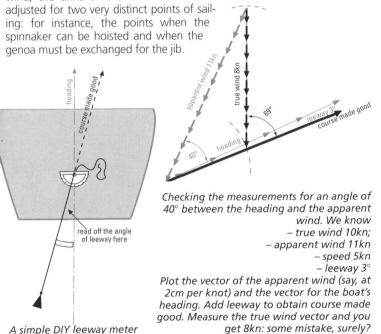

read off the angle of leeway here

A simple DIY leeway meter

Checking the measurements for an angle of 40° between the heading and the apparent wind. We know
– true wind 10kn;
– apparent wind 11kn
– speed 5kn
– leeway 3°
Plot the vector of the apparent wind (say, at 2cm per knot) and the vector for the boat's heading. Add leeway to obtain course made good. Measure the true wind vector and you get 8kn: some mistake, surely?

Estimating the time gained

Let us take the case of a headwind. The diagram on page 160 shows the points that can be reached in the same time by beating lie in a straight line, at right angles to the wind and tangential to the upper

159

edges of the diagram on both sides of the beating sector. The tangential points of the straight line and the diagram indicate precisely the best close-hauled course that can be made on either tack.

According to the same principle, it is possible to know all the targets that can be reached in the same time by tacking on either side of a stern wind. All are situated on a straight line tangential to the curve of the diagram. This straight line – called the isochrone – allows for an exact evaluation to be made of the amount of time one gains in relation to the course that would have been run by taking the direct route. Its tangential points with the curve also show which are the best reaching angles.

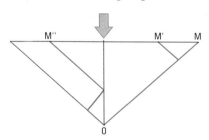

OM = OM' = OM". Starting from O, all points that can be reached within the same time by beating are situated on a line at right angles to the wind direction.

For all points of sailing where the direct route is the fastest, the isochrone naturally merges with the polar curve. It is time to see what conclusions come out of this in practice, first in a steady wind, and then when a change in the wind is expected.

Reaching

You are in the vicinity of the buoy SN 1, off the mouth of the Loire, and you are making for Belle-Île. The wind is light from the SW. Your boat is making 5kn, and you are engaged in pondering over the eternal question: to fly or not to fly the kite. You do not know your boat very well. On the other hand, trying out the spinnaker seems like a fun idea, and it seems as if you could carry one on the present point of sailing. Up goes the spinnaker, but alas, it turns out to be a mistake, as it doesn't pull well and the boat does not go any faster. You decide to bear away slightly so that the spinnaker will be of some use after all.

Bearing away by 10°, things go rather better. The spinnaker is pulling correctly, the speed is 6kn and everything is just wonderful. Nevertheless, you look at the chart to see where this departure from the straight and narrow is taking you. You notice that the difference is not great and you can happily carry on like this for a while. Since the boat is going a bit faster, there will be no real loss.

At this point you notice that the gain in speed is actually quite considerable, given the comparatively small extra distance that will have to be covered. If you decide to make half the trip with the spinnaker, and then head directly for Kerdonis, you will have only added

160

Reaching.
The course to be made is 290°. On this course, it would be impossible to carry the spinnaker; we are making 4kn and will reach point A. If we start out at 279°, hoist the spinnaker and do 4·7kn for half an hour, followed by a turn to 301°, putting on the genoa for the next half hour and make 4kn, then we shall reach point B on the isochrone. The average speed is thus 4·25kn, or 6% more than by the direct route. If we wanted to make the best speed with the spinnaker, we would actually be travelling more slowly: half an hour on a bearing of 270° at 5kn followed by another half an hour on 313° at 6kn would only take us to point C.

1·5% to the journey while your speed will have increased by 20% over this part of the voyage; in fact, you could quite easily do more than half the trip under spinnaker and you would still gain. You will finish the journey on a close reach, a point of sailing on which your speed will be little different from the one you were making on the direct route, and you will be in Kerdonis much earlier than you thought.

If the forecast announces that the wind is going to back southerly you will be able to make the entire trip under spinnaker. If the wind is going to veer north, then it is probably better, given your lack of experience, to do the first part of the journey on a close reach. In order to know when you could then put on the spinnaker and head for Kerdonis you would have to know at what wind angle your spinnaker would become effective, and then trace on the chart a line from Kerdonis which represents your course at that angle and then join this course on a close reach.

In fact if the wind is due to increase, it is better, given your lack of experience, to give up the idea of the spinnaker and head off by the direct route. Caution counsels you not to move from the direct course unless you are going to profit from it in some immediate way. In any case you ought to estimate how much the wind angle will change, and when. If you think you will reach Belle-Île before the strong wind, try your luck with the spinnaker up, but bear in mind that you might end up entering the port close-hauled. It's up to you.

Now, there are less rough-and-ready methods than the ones you are using at the moment. If you are sailing near the SN1 buoy and you see a racing yacht pass head down, round the buoy and then break out the spinnaker in double-quick time, taking off on the correct course without blinking, then you can be sure there is an expert navigator on board who does not waste time worrying about the metaphysics of spinnakers.

Well before they reached the SN1 buoy, that navigator took out

161

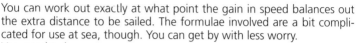

You can work out exactly at what point the gain in speed balances out the extra distance to be sailed. The formulae involved are a bit complicated for use at sea, though. You can get by with less worry.
You need to know:
■ the distance AB;
■ the velocity of the boat V over the direct route AB (and thus the time it would take direct);
■ the angle a between the direct route and the detour;
and the gain in speed ΔV resulting from the detour.
Assuming that the second part of the route (CB) may also be sailed at the same velocity V, you can then work out t1, the length of time for which it is worthwhile sailing away from the direct course, under spinnaker. The formula is:

$$t1 = \frac{AB}{\Delta V} \times \cos a \left(\frac{V + \Delta V - V}{\Delta V + 2V} \right)$$

In practice, we can simplify things. Since it is a question of small angles, we can treat cos a as 1. The formula is then:

$$t1 = \frac{AB}{\Delta V + 2V}$$

In our example:
■ the distance AB is 24 nautical miles;
■ the boat would sail 5kn on the direct course, and would take 4hr 48min to cover it;
■ angle a is 10° and the gain in speed ΔV is 1kn.
The time t1 for which you should carry the spinnaker is thus:

$$t1 = \frac{24}{1 + 10} = 2hr\ 11min$$

which at 6kn gives us 13·1 nautical miles.

his polar diagram for today's conditions, drawn on tracing paper so he could lay it on the chart, centring it on the buoy and orientating it according to the wind. You can be certain that he has immediately decided on the best course to follow, and what the gain will be in speed and time. He's probably feeling pretty pleased with himself. Each to his own.

Downwind
Here the tactic is very simple, as we know. You go faster by tacking downwind than by running straight before the wind.
    You can be quite satisfied with a rough estimate of the best broad reach (the point of sailing that will give you the best speed for the least detour). However, it is also possible to estimate more pre-

cisely without too much of a strain. With the wind astern (and only with the wind astern) the true and apparent wind are in the same direction.

We know that if your diagram is to be of any use then it must show the true wind, so all you have to do is place yourself dead downwind, log the compass course and speed, then luff up nice and gently, continuing to record the speed every 5°.

In a very short time you will know which is the very best angle of broad reach, for that particular wind strength at least. Even if you don't go so far as to make a diagram, these things can be noted in a corner of the log book for future use. Should you make short dog legs or long dog legs? Everything depends on what the wind is going to do. If the wind is unlikely to change direction, or you don't know, then it is probably best to make small dog legs (even though you might actually lose a little time gybing).

If you move off the direct route too far, then it only takes a small shift of wind at the last minute for you to have to run the last part with the wind dead astern, which would wipe out all the benefits gained from tacking downind. However, if you have not moved far from your direct course, then a shift of wind will either have no effect or be beneficial – unless it is more than 80°, in which case you will have to take down the spinnaker. When a change in direction of this magnitude is forecast, then you must give up all idea of tacking downwind, and immediately get on the course that will be imposed on you by the wind backing or veering: in other words, luff up in the direction from which the wind is expected.

Beating

How can you improve on a course when your destination lies in the direction the wind is coming from? Here the question of wind strategy takes a peculiar turn: the boat is closehauled, and it is no longer a question of whether a detour will result in better progress to windward since, by definition, sailing closehauled provides that progress; as long as the wind does not shift, the question is easily answered.

Headwind theorem

Let us take several identical boats, all making 50° to windward. They are spread out on a line m–n and are preparing to beat towards point A. The angle xAy, bisected by the axis of the wind, is equal to the beating sector: 100°.

The important thing is that all the boats on the line m–n are at an equal distance from A, once their tacks are taken into account.

We can verify from the diagram overleaf that two boats setting out from D and tacking differently would cover the same distance to get to A, and that at any point on the course (eg D′ and D″) their progress would be identical. Conversely, any boats to the left of B or

163

the right of C are further away and will take longer to get there.

Close-hauled, the shortest course lies within an angle equal to the beating sector whose bisector is the axis of the wind; all courses within this angle are at an equal distance from A.

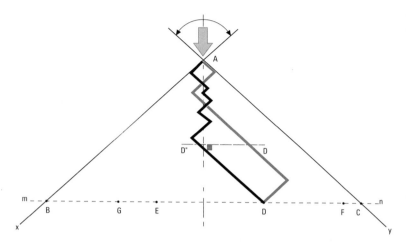

Taking account of all the tacks to be made, all the boats on the line m–n and in the sector xAy are at an equal distance from A.

Shifting wind theorem

Now the wind backs 15°, and everything changes. The new beating angle is x'Ay', and the projection of each boat onto the bisector shows that E is now nearest to A, followed by D, F and C. B is well and truly out of the running. There is some doubt about G, which lies outside the beating angle but slightly to windward of E. If we suppose, to take an example, that G is the boat on which the earlier diagrams were based, then it would gain an extra 11% in speed for an extra 9·5% of route…

The distance of the boats from their objective has also changed, except for D. It is 21% less for E, 24% more for F and 56% more for C. One can imagine that the morale must have changed quite a bit on the boats D' and D": the distance relative to A has been reduced by 12% for D" and increased by 17% for D'.

These observations add some nuances to the foregoing theorem. If the wind is not going to shift, then tacks can be made in the whole triangle BAC, but in practical terms it is unwise to pursue that theory, because if the wind changes then there is a better than 50% chance of losing out: either by being too far to windward, as with B, or by being too far to leeward, as is the case with D, F and C.

In practice, experience shows that when it is not known if the wind is going to change, whether backing or veering, the

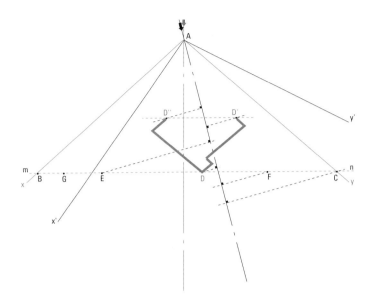

The wind backs 15° and everything changes. This requires some thought.

safest option is to tack within a sector of 10°, with the true wind direction as its axis.

In this context, when the objective does not lie exactly in the eye of the wind, the question arises of the choice of direction for the first tack. This is simply an extension of the previous rule, for it should be apparent that the best tack is the one which brings the boat closest to its objective. In our diagram, it is D" that has made the best tack.

Now, if a change in wind direction is forecast, and if the direction of the change is known, then the situation changes yet again, and we must look back at the diagram: when the change occurs, it is D that is closest to the axis of the wind, but E that wins out. We can therefore deduce the following rule: **When a change in wind direction is forecast, keep to the side from which the wind is going to come.**

The difficulty is to know where to go on that side and which beating sector to adopt. To find the answer, the wind shift must be assessed as accurately as possible. Generally speaking, it can be assumed that the angle between the present direction of the wind and the windward edge of the new beating sector cannot be greater than the difference between the present heading of the boat and the angle of the wind shift predicted. If, for example, the boat is making 45° into the wind and a wind shift of 30° is predicted, then the difference 45° − 30° = 15° indicates that the direction to windward of the new beating sector must be between 5° and 15° off the axis of the present wind, on the side from which the new wind is going to come.

This simple bit of arithmetic throws up another rule: **the greater the shift in the wind is expected to be, the less you should move off the axis of the present wind**. If a wind shift of 40° is forecast, then the calculation 45° − 40° = 5° shows that no change must be made.

Let us return to where we were before, somewhere between the buoy SN1 and Belle-Île. Five identical boats are now making for Kerdonis. The wind is from the NW (wind no 1) and the forecast announces that it is going to veer N. On board each boat, the crews are wondering about the change in the wind, and how they should respond to it.

On board boat A, it is thought that they will have reached Belle-Île before the wind changes. So they continue to beat within the 10° sector (marked in dark colour) with the present wind as its axis.

On board boat B, it is thought that the wind will veer soon and that it will be about 30° different. They therefore make the calculation 45° − 30° = 15°. B makes a long port tack to place itself ready for a beat in the grey sector, between 5° and 15° from the axis of the present wind.

On board boat C, the extent of the change is not discussed. The more to windward, it is argued, the better. C therefore makes a long tack to the NE, not worrying about when they are to go about.

On board boat D, it is thought that the wind will not change much: 45° − 20° = 25°. D sets off to beat in the pale-coloured sector, situated between 15° and 25° from the axis of the wind at present.

On board boat E, it is thought that the wind will change considerably: about 40°, which gives them 45° − 40° = 5°. They decide not to move off the present heading.

Thus, for quite different reasons, boats A and E will stay in the same sector, while the others move in the direction from which the wind will come.

They have all covered 14 nautical miles, when the wind changes by 20° (wind no 2). Let us look at how things now stand. For A and E, the route is shortened by 6%, for B by 11% and for D by 21%. C went too far, moving out of the new beating sector, and a good way to windward of D. C is now 12% further away from the objective than D. The gain in speed (9%) will not compensate for the extra miles added.

It is interesting to see what would have happened with different changes in the wind direction. If the wind shifts by 40° (wind no 4) then the routes of A and E will be shortened by 22%, while B and D, both outside the beating sector, might make up the extra distance through the increase in speed and catch up. C is out of the running: its speed would have to increase by 18% to arrive at the same time as the others. If the wind shifts by 60° (wind no 5) then all the boats will be outside the new beating sector, but A and E are closer to the

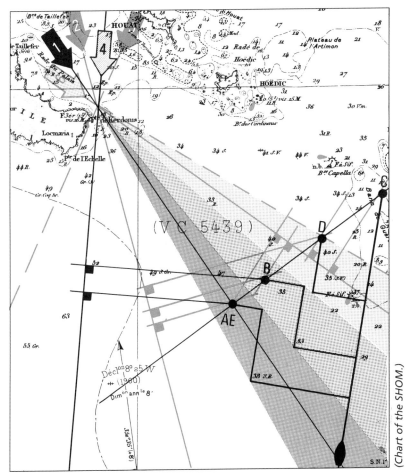

(Chart of the SHOM.)

objective. If the wind backs by about 20° (wind no 6) then C's route increases by 16%, and D's by 10%; B's does not change, while A's and E's decrease by 6%.

From all these results, we can draw the following conclusions:

■ **The winner is the one who predicts the change most accurately.**

■ **The one who chooses the direct route is always well placed, winning in three of the cases (where the wind turns a great deal, where it does not turn, and where it turns in an unexpected direction).**

■ **In all cases, a big detour is worse than useless.**

In several cases, it will have been noticed that there were always boats out of the new beating sector, but to windward of the others, and that these stood a good chance of making up for lost time, since they were heading for the objective on a close fetch and were therefore sailing faster than those close-hauled.

This leads us to consider a special case: when the objective being made for can be laid in one tack close-hauled. In this case, it can be advisable sometimes to bear away a little to gain speed, if a change in the wind is expected before the end of the passage, either because the wind heads you by more than half the boat's heading, or because it frees a little.

Depending on the distance remaining to be covered and the weather forecast, the line of thinking can change entirely. The further away the objective, the greater the chance that the wind will shift during the trip. If a polar front is active over the area, then you should be thinking in terms of what will happen over the next few hours, whereas in a depression it's more a case of what will happen in the next few days. If you get caught in a monsoon, then you're looking more to the long term.

Crossing the Channel

To sum up what we have covered so far, we shall look at how to approach a number of different Channel crossings, in a classic meteorological situation: a depression has just passed and another is on the way. The wind is blowing from the NW and should back soon.

If you are going from the Scilly Isles to Bréhat (course 115°) the direct route obliges you to sail with the wind dead astern – always a bad point of sailing. However, it would be inadvisable to start tacking downwind, since there is a chance of the wind shifting to the point where you could not carry the spinnaker. It is therefore preferable to luff up a little on the starboard tack and keep on it: you will then stand a good chance of making the crossing first on a broad reach and finishing on a reach.

From Torquay to Bréhat (course 169°) the direct route is on a broad reach, but for the same reasons as before, it is better to luff up in the direction from which the wind is going to come. If the forecast is that the wind will change in the first part of the crossing, then it is a good idea to luff up by 15° as soon as you have passed Start Point. If the change in the wind is only going to occur towards the end of the crossing, then you should luff up by only 5°.

From Plymouth to Ushant (course 199°) the direct course is sailed on a beam reach. Here the choice is difficult and it becomes important to know the latitude over which the forecast depression will pass. If it passes to the north, the wind will perhaps back no further than west. The most likely plan then seems to be to luff up as much as possible with the spinnaker from the word go. If the centre of the depression will pass over the Channel, then it is quite probable that the wind will turn south or even SE. In these conditions, bearing away by 15° in relation to the direct route can be a good tactic. Finally, if you think that the wind is going to settle in the SW, the direct course is the best, trying to make sure that you are as near to Ushant as possible when the wind turns against you.

Tidal strategy

Finding the fastest course in a region criss-crossed by tidal streams can be a complicated business. Everything has to be taken into account at once: the wind, the tidal streams and the combination of the two, which can create a completely new series of problems.

The first thing to bear in mind is that a tidal stream is rarely constant: there are areas where the water is moving faster than in others, and even back eddies. The trick is therefore to find the fast area when the stream is in your favour, and the slow area or back eddy when it is foul. When entering the Channel, for example, along the English coast, remember that the stream is generally weaker out to sea than next to the various headlands along the route: Start Point, Portland Bill, St Albans Head, etc. It is therefore advantageous to keep close to the coast during the flood, and to move out to sea during the ebb (either that or go into the bays). These tactics will gain you faster progress than any straight line.

The problem becomes more complex when you are caught in rectilinear streams, with flow in two opposing directions. It looks as if you can get no advantage from a cross-current but it would certainly appear that you can lose out by struggling against it. This topic has already been touched upon: it is the difference between the course made good over the bottom and the course sailed through the water. If you attempt to keep the course straight over the bottom, you end up sailing a greater distance through the water. The water is, after all, the medium in which you are travelling, and you should not needlessly lengthen the journey in this way.

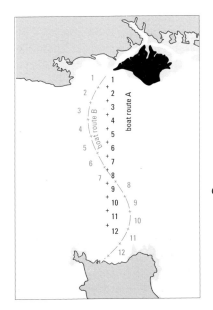

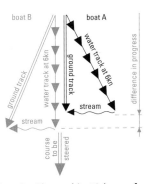

Crossing the Channel in 12 hours from the Solent to Cherbourg. Boat A struggles against the current in order to be able to follow a straight course over the ground. Boat B allows itself to be carried in a sine wave course relative to the bottom, but straight through the water. Despite appearances, this is the faster route.

The example of the Channel crossing illustrated shows that instead of struggling, by letting oneself be carried 6 hours in one direction and then 6 hours in another, keeping a constant heading all the time, the boat follows a sine curve relative to the bottom, but advances in a straight line through the water, and that this is clearly the shortest possible route.

In order to find the shortest possible route in an alternating cross-stream, the principle to follow is always the same: you must total up the streams that you will encounter during the journey, and then displace the point of departure on the chart accordingly. You will then see what heading to keep for the entire trip.

However, the shortest route by this method is not necessarily the fastest, and it might be useful to add a little to the distance in order to get there faster. We must now take account of a new notion, which is the key to subtle navigation in tidal streams: the notion of relative wind.

Relative wind

When a boat enters a tidal stream, the wind changes. As the boat is travelling in a mass of water that is itself moving, the wind that is perceived from the boat is no longer the true wind, but rather a combination of the true wind and the wind due to the speed of the tidal stream. This wind is known as the relative wind. It is not a theoretical force, because it is the wind that creates waves in tidal races and that you feel on board a boat that is drifting in a tidal stream.

When the true wind is strong and the tidal stream weak, then the relative wind is not significantly different from the true wind; but in lighter weather, the difference between the two can become very marked. When a true wind of 5kn, for example, blows against a current of 3kn, then you will feel an 8kn relative wind on board. If the true wind and the current are running in the same direction, then the relative wind will only be 2kn. When the true wind and the current are at an angle to each other (and this is the more common case) then the relative wind differs from the true wind in both strength and direction.

Basic understanding of tidal tactics proceeds from the following observation: since the relative wind depends in part on the stream, its characteristics vary as the stream varies. Therefore, if the variations in stream are predictable, then it must also be possible to predict the resultant winds and take advantage of them.

Geometrical constructions

We meet once again the excellent navigator who had made the passage from the NW Minquiers buoy to Grand-Léjon four times in our earlier chapter. He has kindly agreed to make a fifth trip for us today in conditions very much like the fourth: at spring tides, leaving the

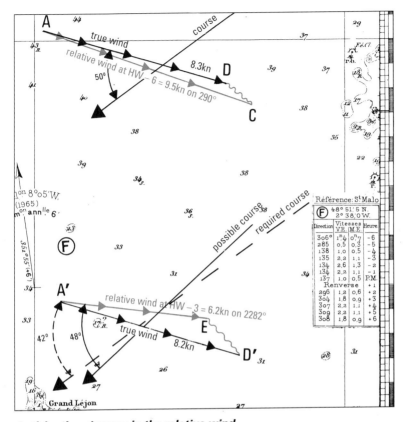

Anticipating changes in the relative wind
Above: from the present relative wind vector AC and the present current vector CD, we derive the true wind vector AD.
Below: from the true wind A'D' and the characteristics of the current ED' at a given hour, we obtain the characteristics of the relative wind for the time in question.
Here we see that the relative wind will drop and head the boat.
(Chart of the SHOM.)

NW Minquiers at HW -6. The only difference is that the wind that was E to start with has come round to the west and has freshened to Force 3.

Our man reckons he can do the passage in about five hours if he doesn't have to tack. He calculates his course in the same way as he did for previous trips, displacing the point of departure by the amount of current he will have under him for those five hours and then works out his true course, correcting for variation and leeway to get his compass course.

He notes that he can make the trip very easily starting at HW -6 and that he can make Grand-Léjon on a close fetch. However, the tide is going to turn in the course of the next few hours, and at HW -3 it will be running at 2·2kn at 135°. So the question arises: when the tide turns, what will be the effect on the relative wind?

In order to see what the resultant wind might be like at HW -3, we will have to know its components, that is to say the true wind and the tidal stream at the time. The characteristics of the tidal streams are already known, but we have to find out the true wind now, and assume that it will not change in the next three hours.

Now, when you are sailing in a tidal stream, it is impossible to measure the true wind unless you anchor first. You work back to the true wind from the relative wind and the current. You calculate the relative wind in the same way that you calculated the true wind when drawing up polar diagrams. Since the characteristics of the stream are known, all that remains to be done is to draw up a bit of simple geometry on the chart. The relative wind is plotted as vector AC, orientated in the same direction as the wind and of a length proportional to its strength (x knots of wind speed = x nautical miles on the chart). At C, you plot the current (vector CD corresponding to 1·4kn at 306°). The true wind is therefore represented by the vector AD.

In order to calculate the relative wind at HW -3, the same sort of operation must be carried out the other way round, that is to say starting from the true wind A'D' and plotting from D' the vector for the stream (2·2kn at 135°). The relative wind is then represented by the vector A'E. Our navigator sees immediately that his fears were well founded: after the tide turns, the wind will drop and head the boat. It will be 34% weaker and 25° further ahead than at present. We shall no longer be able to make the desired course, and we shall have to tack to make Grand-Léjon.

Since that's how it is, the navigator takes the necessary decision straight away. Instead of following the course he had originally planned and sailing on a close fetch from NW of the Minquiers, he will luff up immediately and sail close-hauled. He may therefore be able to lay Grand-Léjon on a single tack and save a good deal of time. He can see from his first calculation that he can make an excellent close-hauled course the moment he leaves, since the relative wind is not so far ahead and is stronger than the true wind. The boat is being pushed closer to the wind by the tide, so he can steer a heading closer to the true wind than if there were no tidal stream. Things are completely reversed three hours later.

Our navigator has kindly been giving us a detailed explanation to show the kind of working that has to go on. Most of the time, it is unnecessary to look in such detail at the relative wind; it is more important to predict how it will change over time. The little tricks we have described will be useful for avoiding confusion at some stage in the future: you simply scribble your precisely calculated vectors approximately on the back of an envelope, taking the stream (your only known vector), working out the present true wind and the expected relative wind, which can be fairly approximate. It will become apparent very quickly whether the wind will free you or head you, drop or freshen.

A check list for choosing your course

■ Trace your proposed route on the chart: does it take you too close to a hazard?
■ Have you got enough water beneath the keel at all times?
■ Is there a stream? How strong? When will it be fair for setting out?
■ What is the wind like? What does the shipping forecast say?
■ Is there a chance of running into a sea raised by the tide against the wind?
■ How long can the crew be expected to stay at sea?
■ Can you sail the route in darkness?
■ Have you got easily identified landmarks?
■ Have you read the relevant pages of the pilot?
■ If you have an accident, is there a sheltered emergency harbour or anchorage?
■ If fog comes, can you still find your way?

INDEX